ALPHABET JAZZ

11/30/24 Duluth MN

To Tony —
Keep up the great work &
long live the red carpet!
[illegible]

ALPHABET JAZZ

Poetry, Prose,
Stories, and Songs

Paul Metsa

Charleston, SC
www.PalmettoPublishing.com

Alphabet Jazz: Poetry, Prose, Stories, and Songs

Editors: Jackie Cheves, Lisa Dahlseid, Maija Jenson, and Annie Possis

Cover design: Mike Goebel

Front cover photograph: Howard Christopherson
of People Places Dreams Photography

Back cover photograph: Scott Streble

Title page drawing: James Wrayge

Guitar and case photo, p. viii: Donald Jay Olson

Printed in the U.S.A
First paperback edition: September 2022

Paperback: 979-8-88590-480-3
eBook: 979-8-88590-481-0

www.paulmetsa.com

CONTENTS

DEDICATION

Alphabet Jazz is dedicated to my dearest friend and favorite poet, Kelly Hotchkiss. We've spent nearly 40 years playing with language like silly putty, sharing ideas, favorite books and songs, and inspiration like some guys trade baseball cards.

He's always been in my corner, holding my hand in moments of terror, bucking me up when I was less than sure of myself, and waving my pirate flag as a true believer. I hope I've done the same for him.

If God could make a better, or funnier, drinking buddy, She hasn't done so yet. And you don't have to take my word for it. He was also my beloved mother's favorite friend of mine. I rest my case.

Kelly Hotchkiss and Paul Metsa
New Port Richey, Florida, 2019
(Photo by Mary Hotchkiss)

This book is also dedicated to my dear mother, Bess Metsa. She was my biggest fan and supporter, driving me to my first gigs until I got my driver's license. The last time she saw me play was my sold-out show, with a 10-piece band, at the Guthrie Theater in Minneapolis on January 31, 1994. She looked like the happiest mom in the world that evening. She passed away on May 23, 1994. I miss her like the meadow would miss the wind and rain.

Bess Margaret (Paul) Metsa
August 25, 1929 – May 23, 1994
(Photo by Walter Paul)

ACKNOWLEDGMENTS

Indiegogo Supporters: Linda O'Leary, Doug Ellis, Janet Bayliss, Gary Popovich, Marc Percansky, Jennifer Bonner, Eve Peckenpaugh, Chelsy Whittington, Karan Skarja, Charles Trittin, Thomas Johnson, Rubin Latz, Brian Drake, John Kiriakou, Maureen Heinen, Todd Rolfson, and Jeff Forester.

Special Thanks: Jackie Cheves, Amy Hawkins Donlin, Piper Donlin Anderson, Andy and Priscilla Watson, Pat Dwyer, Bruce Wilson, Josh Horwitz, Michael Tearson, Kevin Odegard, Cray McCally, Todd Orjala, Keith Balke, Terry Carlson, Marido Huber, Steve Baker, Paul Mandell, Cam Strang, Carol Krueger, Yellow Cloud, and Lynn Hall and the Michelob Golden Girls.

Roadside Assistance: Jack and Laura, Denny Mo and Laura, Coy and Ank, Booka and Edythe, Joe and Melanie, Jeff and Rosie, Kelly and Mary, Billy and Tara, Sonny and Lesa, Jef and Molly, Izzy Wilson, Judy Walker, Metsa family, Cheves family, Axtell family, Donna Wright, Jerry Disrud, Baby Grant Johnson, Nora Guthrie, Steve Karras, Arne Brogger, Phil Freshman, Duane Arens and MCN6, Chad Larson and AM 950, Pat Courtemanche, Rick Shefchik, Harvey Van Horn, Marcus Johnson, Bob McNamara, Bill Pagel, Annie Possis, Lisa Dahlseid, Scotty Herold, Jeff and Scott Asbach, Jean Cole (Hometown Focus), and Cheri Friedman.

Heavenly Hall of Fame: Elder and Bess Metsa and Betty Hawkins.

FOREWORD

I met Paul Metsa in the mid-sixties. We lived in the same town on Minnesota's Iron Range and attended the same grade school. He was one of the few guys who came to grade school with a guitar, which was very cool at that time. We were at the tail end of the "folk scare," the beginning of "folk rock," and the airwaves were filled with words and music. Formative times for folks like us. Later, in high school, he was known as an all-around creative type, a guy with eyes open and willing to take a chance. He played in a popular band called Damn Everything But the Circus, the name borrowed from an e.e. cummings poem, indicating both poetic appreciation and decent attendance in English class.

As the years went on, he moved to Minneapolis, traveled the world, and established himself over the course of four decades as a formidable musician and a gifted singer-songwriter. He became an author with the publication of his book *Blue Guitar Highway*, and now makes his poetry debut with this collection, *Alphabet Jazz*. But the poetic has been there all along with Paul.

You don't write songs without a knack for poetry, you don't write books without a way with words, and you don't entertain folks for forty years without a great feel for the narrative, the punchline, and the flow. Here is what I hear in this collection: I hear wind through northern pines, the chimes of decades changing; I hear the Beat Poets and The Byrds; I hear the other poet from down the road in Hibbing; I hear loves lost and found, and I hear that English class.

They say that all poets stand on the shoulders of their English teachers. Paul's English teacher, Tommy Moeller, played a Stratocaster in a Chisholm rock band and got a master's in English taking a class from B. J. Rolfzen, who happened to be Bob Dylan's high school English teacher, whom that 2018 Nobel Prize in Literature recipient called his "single greatest influence." Take what you have gathered from that coincidence...

I remember the day that I first realized Paul Metsa was a poet. Back in 1975, the Eldorado Bar on Chestnut Street in our hometown of Virginia, Minnesota, served as the main office for those of us hitting the perfect trifecta of music, irresponsibility, and misspent youth. Over cold beers one afternoon, he laid a haiku-type poem on me as the guilty summer sun filtered through the barroom window. It went something like this:

Good hash puts a ring in your ears

Good whiskey makes you forget about beer

Time goes slow, just count the years

A good Kleenex will dry those tears

Maybe it was the times, maybe It was the Iron Range, or maybe it was that English class. In the touchscreen world we now inhabit, poetry still has a place, and words still matter. So, enjoy this cool collection of writings, listen to the man, and dig the flow.

John Pasternacki
November 3, 2021

PREFACE

Alphabet Jazz is a collection of poetry, prose, stories, and songs I wrote between 1984 and 2022. It started coming together in 2020 as I was preparing to move out of Minneapolis, my home since 1978.

The anthology is a personal diary of sorts—midnight blasts of inspiration, love letters as poems, personal tributes, true stories, letters to editors and friends, and songs that I have written along the way and still perform. My two talented rescue dogs, Blackie (RIP) and Blue, each contribute a piece as well. Overall, it is also my valentine to Minneapolis, where over the course of 40 years, I found inspiration and friendship in every corner of town.

Support your local humane shelters. My two favorites are
Contented Critters (Blackie)
https://www.contentedcrittersmn.org/

and Heart of Alabama: Save, Rescue, Adopt (Blue)
https://www.hasradog.org/

"The beauty of obscurity is you never go out of style."

Paul Metsa

MEMO FROM REGO PARK

A dog whistle wind night
paint spray on disappearing street
Arpeggio vapor trail and
a bleach blonde discount

Trini Lopez and family, too
two– or three–chord Monte Hall
behind doors numbered two and three

Give the Chevy Nova to someone who cares or needs it
With Civil War alibis, cattle car algebra
Lone street song
Homeless Albert on a borrowed harp
baby blue Cadillacs and matching lingerie

Lonesome chorus
hallelujah bunk bed
Good night poems
Ivory trinket lullaby
Last trick ponies for wee small children
on the subways of the damned

Blue light echoes
static volume curtain call

Mae East or West
and someone named Frenchy when you least need him

Forgive but don't forget, apply but don't return
For they've taken all your numbers away
Gave you a Spanish alphabet, nicknames, and a joke book
Babysitter's west coast dream

Cast iron ukuleles
semi-permanent straw hat
Tin star promise
and someone else's name
In the witness protection program
of your choice

Buy, you need more, what else is new?
Straight circle overcoat
bad moustache
No bungalow for Romeo
flophouse magazines
Lemon tongue promise
a missed kiss or two
Car keys and a razor blade

Hoping we'd have more to show for this
Raise your hand in a moment of
silence
But don't cease to dream
For they can't steal that
in our irregular moments of grace

PAPER TIGERS

Justice is done when poor sheriff gets his fee
Pay the fiddler double-time only prisoners sing for free
Dead dreams swing on show-biz black sharkskin
Head up downstreet G-men sell you poison gin

Chorus

It's only paper tigers
It's only paper tigers
It's only paper tigers

Hawked the wigwam shaker spirit midnight coal
Electric Jesus got his neon stripped and kicked parole
Basket man burns papoose full of perfumed owls
Sawed off shepherd left the black sheep out to howl

Repeat Chorus

Blood monkey shiver, straight jacket overcoat
Invisible army is peeking through the holes
Candy cane kisses lost on losing lips
Double-crosses for the Missus, single file while the honey drips

Repeat Chorus

Pretty pennies can't buy back lost time sight unseen
Wolverines surround the wagons uptown cowgirl's dream
Dynamite the doorbell let someone paint all the windows
    Black
Sneak out the alley bag lady autographs the gunny sack

Repeat Chorus

Words and Music by Paul Metsa
Paul Metsa Music – 1984 – BMI ©

LARRY KEGAN

He Was a Friend of Mine

♦ *A Tribute* ♦

Editor's Note: Singer-songwriter Larry Kegan died Tuesday morning, September 11, 2001, of cardiac arrest at the age of 59. A diving accident left Kegan a paraplegic when he was only 16 years old, and 10 years later he became a quadriplegic from a car accident. Yet Kegan later wrote in a song, "Every misfortune can be a blessing in disguise."

He met Bob Dylan when they were teenagers at summer camp and the two became close friends for life. Dylan's first recording was comprised of songs he performed with Kegan and others. Dylan dedicated his Street Legal album to Kegan. Kegan first performed with Bob Dylan in concert on October 19, 1981, in Merryville, Indiana, singing "No Money Down" while Dylan played saxophone. In 1997, Dylan saluted to him from the stage at Midway Stadium in St. Paul, Minnesota.

A few years ago, On the Tracks magazine spoke with Kegan requesting an interview. After a few days of careful deliberation, he decided to kindly decline because he didn't want to risk jeopardizing his lifelong friendship with Dylan.

Larry Kegan was a steel-wheeled high street hipster; a saint who shook, rattled, and rolled up to the very end. He was born and is now buried in St. Paul, Minnesota, just a stone's roll away from the Mississippi River, right before it floors it along Hwy 61 down to the Big Easy and becomes saltwater.

He was halfway through his victory lap toward his 60th birthday before his 3D heart gave out on him in the van and on the road. He was with his driver, on the way to the record shop to pick up a new platter about love and robbery. This, just hours after two towers crumbled in Manhattan and ripped the heart out of the rest of us. As was his style, King Kegan, as I fondly called him, spent most of that morning calling all his New York City pals, making sure they were alright. Even though he spent the last 45 years of his life confined to a wheelchair, he used a psychic radar to track the trails of those fortunate to be his friends, uplifting us when needed with an abundant grace of spirit, old-world wisdom, humor, and prayer. His was a sixth sense born through the blood drops of struggle.

Though he left this world as he arrived – a chosen leader of the tribe – he was, for a little while, just another teenager in Eisenhower's America, deep in the heart of the wild Midwest. Little Richard, Doo Wop, Marlon Brando and Chuck Berry, Bugs Bunny, and Bugsy Siegel all within spittin' distance of Frankie Laine, spilling into those St. Paul nights where boys whistled at the girls and the girls whistled back. Come all ye fair and tender maidens to these make-believe ballrooms, for the moon is out and beckons us to dance.

Kegan spent his first 16 years on two feet in a world that never stopped spinning. But it stopped twice for him. Once in a diving accident in 1958 that stole the use of his legs, and then on a Mexican road at midnight when he was 25, in a car accident that would eventually lay claim to all movement below the neck. Sentenced at midnight to a life in a wheelchair – as he would write about later in a blues howl called "Some Get the Chair," a tune that would make Harlan Howard proud, Mother Maybelle in the air.

I met him in the early '80s on the banks of the river. His reputation preceded him – a Gary Cooper High Noon shadow of whispers. Word had it that he was summer camp buddies with another local Jewish kid, one from the red dust mines of Minnesota's Iron Range, one who went on to make quite a name for himself channeling the still-living spirit of Woody Guthrie.

They were pals like Tom and Huck, first hooked on the 50,000-watt late-night border radio broadcasts that spread that gutbucket Negro howl all over the White heartland. Now we call it early rock and roll, but back then it was just the real America, unseen and Top of the World, Ma. From the downbeat, Kegan seemed as interesting, mysterious, and powerful as his soon-to-be very famous friend. And 'til the end, he was the best friend that Iron Range rounder ever had.

Kegan had had his ass kicked from sea to shining sea. Yet, playing the hand God dealt him, he rolled 7's on tilted tables from Tijuana to Times Square. Midnight rambles, prayer meetings, rock and roll shows, emergency rooms, classrooms, red desert highways, winding rivers and sky-blue water lakes, Quonset huts, boardrooms and bordellos – Kegan knew them all. He swung with the best of 'em, took on all comers, never backed down, and never once felt sorry for himself, nor let you feel sorry for yourself. His was a high-octane spirit world and his heartbeat for everyone. Body be damned, say a prayer and be brave like Lenny Bruce – it is Saturday night, after all.

He could enter a room like Liz Taylor – head held high, dressed in a coat of many colors – wheeled through the doorway by his Mexican mafia, his personal attendants who kept him on the road, brimming with a dignity that he was always willing to share. Hello, Stranger. And in the last ten years, usually within love's glance of Carol Krueger, first his nurse and then the true love of his life, and the best friend he ever had.

A natural born storyteller, Old Testament style. He'd command a stage in a way that would make Miles Davis proud, except Kegan never turned his back on the audience. Blues shouter, poet, songwriter, author, speaker, student, scholar, son, brother, lover, father, and friend. And such a friend - a friend to you, your friends, and their friends. Everyone is equal in the eyes of God.

You are blessed once with the love of your mother when you enter this world. You are blessed twice when you find a friend who'll love you like your mother did. Larry Kegan was that kind of friend, the finest God sees fit to give someone. To say it was an honor to know him would understate how I actually feel. I believe he was put on this earth to show the rest of us the power and strength of the human spirit. A Jericho blast of flesh and bone, honor and dignity, beauty, and truth.

At his funeral service, not quite 24 hours after the horror of the morning of 9/11, the rabbi supposed that God might have called Larry to heaven to help all those disabled victims make their transition to the spirit world. I can't doubt this. I do know that when I dream about him, he is dancing. After 45 years, out of that chair and dancing.

Paul Metsa (with the help of Joe Gioia)
On the Tracks, September 2002

Willie Murphy, Larry Kegan, and Paul Metsa
(Photo by Mike Rivard)

WHISTLING PAST THE GRAVEYARD

Do not play with matches
'Cause matches will start a fire
Keep your foot above flames
When walking on the wire
Life is sweet but time is short
Keep your train on the track
When you're whistling past the graveyard and
        The graveyard whistles back.

Don't forget your mother
She brought you in this world
You are the dream that she once had
Since she was just a little girl
Send her cards and flowers
Don't step on the crack
When you're whistling past the graveyard and
        The graveyard whistles back.

The world don't owe you nothing
Don't even know your name
You might be a king or queen
But the end treats you just the same
Drop your crumbs before you leave
Don't cover up your tracks
When you're whistling past the graveyard and
        The graveyard whistles back.

Someday you may lose your true love
To a stranger in a crowd
Same old story for a thousand years
That makes you cry out loud

But one day she'll find that stranger
Is just a con man in a gunny sack
When she's whistling past the graveyard and
        The graveyard whistles back.

Go to your confession
Read your horoscope
Tell a white lie to a rabbi
Make a collect call to the Pope
But the faith that will save you
May also break your back
When you're whistling past the graveyard and
        The graveyard whistles back.

You might be in a wheelchair
Or have to step so light
Around the world in 80 days
At the speed of light
Everything that is given to you
May one day be taken back
When you're whistling past the graveyard and
        The graveyard whistles back.

Words and Music by Paul Metsa
Paul Metsa Music – 1992 – BMI ©

WHISPERED NOTE BETWEEN STRANGERS

Even the bell of midnight needs a night off
now and then
The moon goes in and out on its own time

Keeps it all to himself
(I will share, of course, with friends
but sometimes friends are hard to find
and this night might be one of those)

With a jug half full of wine and an alley full of nothing
anything or everything is possible
In stillness, time is almost out of reach
Daylight just round the corner, at least let's hope so

No angles or the jingle jangle bells of morning
Dawn's all grey, and nothing but forgiving
and when it casts its glance to the judge's chair
let's hope to God he is asleep
In sleep and dreams we all become equal

In sleep and in dreams we become who we are
In beauty, grace, and the rusted sunshine of all promises
that were promised to no one, but in noon's honest light are
welcome to all

I'll take it, throw buffalo nickels to dead-end kids
and lend dollars to pinstripe men and women
with kids at home
for even those of us without them would do the same

For those of us with God, and those of us without
at the end of a darkened day can agree
to at least feed the hungry mouths and hearts
that heard we were near and had something to give
that heard our beating hearts and wanted to dance
that knew we had blood like their own
and could share our liquid heart

DYLAN – STILL A HEP CAT

Although Bob Dylan certainly needs no one to defend him, I still take issue with Burl "Ives" Gilyard's shallow musings and cavalier dismissal of the modern Jewish troubadour. His story (The Traveling Wilbury, 8/26/92) contained a series of cheap shots typical of the most quasi-hip channel-surfing music critic.

He hastily concludes Dylan's forte is not live performances after seeing him at the Hubert Humphrey Metrodome and the St. Paul Riverfest. Those formats are akin to seeing a Boris Spassky chess demonstration at the Mall of America. Who wouldn't be a bit shaken by being trapped in a Teflon prison with 50,000 acid-soaked Deadheads with the acoustics of your basic air hangar? And Riverfest will be Riverfest whether it is Dylan or an MTV track show. His forte is the 2-3,000 seat theater where the subtleties of his performance come out.

Sure, Dylan may not be as prolific in his later years as he was during his initial creative surge, but to dismiss anything after *Blood on the Tracks* is complete balderdash. Dylan is both an experiment and testament to whether rock & roll will survive middle age. Though not always graceful, I believe you either accept rock & roll as a viable, breathing, evolving form of American music, or you don't.

Embarrassingly, Gilyard asks the sniveling question, "Why bother?" Could it be perhaps the man just likes to play and it also happens to be how he makes his living? After writing more than 500 songs, destroying Tin Pan Alley, creating an entirely new form of the American popular song – and perhaps changing America in the process – maybe we could give Dylan both respect and the benefit of the doubt. Let him strap on his Stratocaster and let him play whatever he likes. You don't have to see God and it doesn't have to change your life, but what is wrong with luxuriating in the power of pure poetry with a cat who was obviously born to rock & roll, and still does.

Letter to the editor, City Pages,
Minneapolis, September 10, 1992

A FAREWELL TO BILL HINKLEY

◆ *A Tribute* ◆

"The best music is played without pretension."

I am not sure they make men like Bill Hinkley anymore. The patriarch and godfather of Minneapolis' West Bank music scene, Hinkley was a master musician, an Air Force veteran who spoke five languages (including Greek and Mandarin Chinese), a self-taught multi-instrumentalist, a human jukebox of thousands of songs, a storyteller, teacher, sit-down comedian, historian, hero, devoted lover-then-husband to Judy Larson for five decades, and mentor and friend to hundreds of musicians and thousands of fans.

He was both Will Rogers with a mandolin and a philosopher king who held sway in saloons, concert halls, on radio shows, around campfires and kitchen tables, at festivals and benefits – the kind of American who defines this country, and one I was honored to call my friend.

Hinkley, who died Tuesday at age 67, had been fighting a blood disorder for the past couple of years that sapped his strength but never his love for music or his God-given calling to entertain and enlighten with his encyclopedic knowledge of music – in all styles, from every country and in all time signatures.

As a performer he swung and improvised with an abandon that reminded one of Joe Venuti, Django Reinhardt, or the Mississippi Sheiks. He could quote anyone from Shakespeare to Dick Tracy. He had a sense of humor that recalled, at turns, the likes of Mark Twain, H. L. Mencken, or Lord Buckley. And believe me, you have not lived until you've heard Bill Hinkley and Judy Larson sing "Amazing Grace" to the melody of the "Gilligan's Island" theme. Simply brilliant.

A Twin Cities musician friend referred to Hinkley as "our Socrates." Witnessing the dozens of friends who made the pilgrimage to Hinkley's hospice at the Minneapolis Veterans Medical Center—most with instruments in hand, to serenade and play with him when he was able—confirmed that. It was a folkies' Nordic Viking ritual to bid farewell to the king.

As we assembled there in the community room on May 20, right before dinner, the wheelchairs of disabled vets rolled in. You could sense a solidarity with one of their own – brothers in arms, enjoying the fruits and flowering of their service and sacrifice via Brother Bill.

I recently learned that Hinkley attended the same St. Louis grade school as John Hartford, the Mississippi River banjo virtuoso. This makes perfect sense. Both were masters steeped in the grand tradition of folk music, and they shared an abiding love for American culture, music, and history. They passed on that love and knowledge to a couple of generations of musicians. It is now our obligation to do the same.

Hinkley's greatest lessons to me were distilled in two simple concepts: "End every story with a smile or a laugh," and "the best music is played without pretension."

While Hinkley and Larson never got rich playing folk music —he was never in the music business, but rather was in the business of making music, a servant to the song —all of us got richer listening to them play.

Minneapolis Star Tribune, May 10, 2010

Bill Hinkley
(Photo by Joey McLeister)

JACK RUBY

Chorus

Jack Ruby, Jack Ruby in a Cavanaugh hat,
whoever taught you to shoot a pistol like that
Oh, you snuck in the basement and you stood in the back,
Jack Ruby, Jack Ruby in a Cavanaugh hat

Jack Ruby, Jack Ruby when you were fifteen years old
On the south side of Chicago, you looked up to Capone,
Stole girls' lunch money beat boys on their way home
Jack Ruby, Jack Ruby when you were fifteen years old

Jack Ruby, Jack Ruby when you were twenty-one,
You traded brass knuckles for a caliber gun,
In the Sherman hotel bootleg whiskey did run
Jack Ruby, Jack Ruby when you were twenty-one

Jack Ruby, Jack Ruby when you were thirty-five,
set up shop in Dallas had nothing to hide,
a nightclub with hookers and cops side by side
Jack Ruby, Jack Ruby when you were thirty-five

Jack Ruby, Jack Ruby when you were forty-nine,
at the Carousel Club you kept the judges in line,
J. Edgar Hoover said there's no organized crime
Jack Ruby, Jack Ruby when you were forty-nine

Repeat Chorus

Did the Kingfish in New Orleans give you the key?
the numbers to contact the men you should see,
a confederate cloak of conspiracy,
with an eye towards November 1963

When the motorcade turned on Houston and Elm,
Into the crossfire where Camelot fell
Were the shots from the bushes or 6th floor window well? In
Dealey Plaza more than three empty shells

Was Lee Harvey Oswald the only one?
What of those in the bushes who started to run
With secret service credentials and government guns,
They'd answer no questions for what they had done

Oswald was set up, so he did say
before he appeared in the basement driveway
On live television Ruby blew his soul away,
Godspeed the witness with something to say

Repeat Chorus

Jack Ruby, Jack Ruby when you were sixty-four, told Dorothy
Kilgallen you'd even the score,
from your jail cell gave names and numbers and more,
in forty-eight hours, she lay dead on the floor
Jack Ruby, Jack Ruby come back from the grave,
tell us for real whose lives you would save
And the powers behind the deals that were made,
how a President's murder became your stock-in-trade

For those who are guilty are alive to this day,
Got their visas in D.C. and got on their way,
Others laid low until election day,
It was a day of high treason and a quick getaway

Did the Warren Commission mean what they say?
Did the mob or oil money get in the way?
Did the shadow of Cuba darken the day?
In Dallas County the land of LBJ
In Dallas County the land of LBJ

Repeat Chorus

Words and Music by Paul Metsa
Paul Metsa Music – 1992 – BMI ©

MORNING POEM

Ask Studs Terkel where the line between work
and life is drawn
Even he couldn't tell you
nor would he want to

One song ends and another begins
and you can play them both on the same guitar
that sounds better when borrowed
but best when given away

Angels dance in alleys and sometimes
never dance at all

Main Street, at its best, has been all about madness
That is why they call it Main Street

The moon hovers over not because it has to but because it
wants to
Morning comes eventually
over lakes, rivers, cities, and between trees soon to
fall down
because the water tells that story
It sounds like ringing in our ears
It sounds like cathedral bells
and ambulances and cop cars
But eventually when the coffee gets cold
it sounds like ourselves
and we realize we sound
like everybody else

SUE MCLEAN

◆ A Tribute ◆

"Live music is good for the soul."

Sue McLean did more for my career than anybody I've ever had the pleasure of working with. After seeing a transcendent Leo Kottke show at the Guthrie Theater in December of 1972, and deciding that night while driving back through a snowstorm to the Iron Range that I was going to become a professional musician, my only goal was to play the Guthrie. From 1982 until 1994, when I sold it out with a 10-piece band, graced by the presence of my parents (it would be the last time my mother would ever see me play), I played there eight times, and every show was booked by Ms. Sue McLean, one of the greatest independent promoters in the country. Through her grace, I was able to open shows for Ry Cooder with Cats Under the Stars, and opened solo for Lyle Lovett, Roseanne Cash, the Neville Brothers, Leon Russell and Edgar Winter, J.J. Cale, and played other concerts as a participant. Standing on that stage, in the same spot as Miles Davis, the Grateful Dead, the Temptations, the Who, Patti Smith, Sun Ra, Leo Kottke, Bruce Springsteen, the Band, and dozens of others representing the greatest American and international musicians, in a room with pristine acoustics, felt like being in the sound hole of the world's largest guitar, if not in the hand of God himself. And I owe it all to Suzie McLean, a fearless booker, and one of my dearest friends.

She grew up in Dayton, Minnesota, and was a bit of a wild child. Dayton had fewer than 500 people, was three blocks wide and six blocks long, and was surrounded on three sides by two rivers. I imagine her sitting by the banks of those rivers, dreaming of the world to come. I can also imagine her, the only girl in junior high to enjoy an occasional pack of cigarettes, like the protagonist in the song "Leader of the Pack" – which she would truly become. Over the years, she became one of the finest, and one of the first and few, female promoters in America, blasting against the headwinds of the male- dominated world of music, kicking ass and taking names, breaking one glass ceiling after another. And unlike most of the men in the business, she did it with grace, empathy, and humility, and with a true love for the music and, especially in my case, the musicians.

I've said for years you could give Jesus a gig booking a nightclub, and within weeks he'd become a complete jerk. Not Suzie. She booked her first gig in 1974, booking the Suicide Commandos, the first punk band in the Twin Cities, at a high school dance. This totally cut against the grain, as most bands playing those shows would cover songs like "Nights in White Satin" for the young lovers, swinging their partners round and round under the watchful eyes of parents, teachers and chaperones. But like most things Sue would do in life, it worked. She never looked back.

She moved to Minneapolis in the mid-70s and got a gig with Schon Productions, where she made her bones, booking both local and national bands, including the likes of REM at Duffy's in South Minneapolis. Her love of talent was surpassed only by her ear for it. She eventually became the main booker for the Guthrie Theater, where she held forth for 15 years as the main talent buyer, keeping a relationship with them until the end. Most every time I played there, my folks would drive down from my hometown of Virginia, Minnesota, get a room in Minneapolis and enjoy the show. I'd always acknowledge them, and they got a sweet round of applause every time. Minneapolis is cool like that.

After the Guthrie, her newly created production agency, Sue McLean and Associates (SMA), partnered with Jeff Arundel's Triad Productions to start Music in the Zoo in 1996. The summer concert series showcases the beautiful Weesner Amphitheater at the Minnesota Zoo, and the stage is now named for her, after her untimely passing in 2012. She was also the Prime Mover in creating the Mill City Music Festival in downtown Minneapolis in the late '90s, where, after dozens of phone calls, personal persuasion, and counting on the karma she had developed over the years, she booked Prince as a headliner, one of her crowning achievements. It was a major score, and Kimberly Gottschalk, one of her longtime lieutenants, told me she said, "We booked FUCKING Prince!"

As a female promoter with cajones the size of Mexico, she always made sure the majority of her staff were female. As a mentor and visionary, she in 1995 established the Basilica Block Party, an annual fundraiser on the grounds of the Basilica of Saint Mary in downtown Minneapolis that has raised hundreds of thousands of dollars for the church. As a leader of the female tribe, she also started Tween Town in 2010, a summer camp for young girls that introduced them to electric guitars, bands, performance, and all those things that inspire them in music and in life. It continues to this day.

Sue's crowning achievement was adopting her daughter Lilly, then two years old and living in Mexico. She was finally a mother, though she had those instincts all along. Imagine being a 52-year-old single woman and dedicating the next chapter of your life to being a mom. She did it with pride and aplomb. Though they only had 14 years together, Lilly just completed her first year of college at Carleton College in Northfield, Minnesota, and made the Dean's List in her first semester. Like mother, like daughter; Sue would be so proud. We all are.

Sue was not only a complete professional; she developed a sense of humor that could only have been shaped by being baptized in the fires of the blood buckets and bone orchards of rock and roll, where most of us came of age. She had a switchblade sense of humor and timing like Jack Benny. On one of our monthly Friday lunches at Bunkers Bar, where she officed above, she told me about one in her string of ne'er-do-well boyfriends and said, "Yea, I thought he was really cool. He had a motorcycle! Until I realized when the snow hit, that was his only means of transportation," ending with a chuckle and gleam in her eye that could light up Times Square.

A few weeks before she passed, we saw each other at the funeral of one of her old paramours, and one of the best blues guitar players in town. She looked frail. I made a few phone calls and found out she was suffering again from cancer, which she had beat just a few years before. She kept it on the down low, like that small-town gal she always was, with humility and dignity, and everything that she was. Once I found out, I called her to make sure she knew how much I loved her, how much she meant to me, and how much she had done for me professionally and personally. We had a most soulful 20-minute conversation and told each other how much we loved each other. She was in a bit of a morphine haze, but shared with me how she was hoping to put together a show with Diana Ross, plotting the next great production. As we said our goodbyes, she reminded me at the end, "By the way, your comps will be at the door Friday at the Fitzgerald Theater for the Sugarman Rodriquez show." A true professional to the very end, her goodness and generosity on display like always. I'll never forget that conversation, or her. She passed away two days later. May she RIP.

Paul Metsa and Sue McLean
(Photo by Jeff Miletich)

WALKIN' IN A WOMAN'S WORLD

Kitty Genovese was walkin' home one night
Stranger on Queens Boulevard asked her for a light
She said no and he struck her down as 38 looked on
Now those 38 still hear her cries since Kitty has passed on

Carin came home from college
With stories of where she's been
In this town ten years ago, she was the homecoming queen
We won't hear those stories now or meet her boyfriend Dave
It was a short walk from the coffee shop to her shallow grave

Chorus

She ain't safe in a straight line
She ain't safe in a round
She ain't safe in an airplane
She ain't safe on the ground
Because my grandma was once just a girl
Well, I won't stop runnin' 'til
I'm walkin in a woman's world

A little girl on the playground
She dreams of growin' up
She might be a fireman
A princess or a cop
Let her be what she wants to be
Let her not pretend let her be a king or queen
Or the next president

Repeat Chorus

Words and Music by Paul Metsa
Paul Metsa Music – 1994 – BMI ©
Dedicated to the memory of Carin Streufert (1972-1991)

ST. LOUIS COUNTY FAIR

It was Saturday night at the midway
a Mardi Gras Midwestern style
I was with my man the Junkboy from Jersey,
a devils cap and Napolean's smile

We had our tea leaves read by Lady Samantha,
she said one of you will fall in love
But the Junkboy had Madame Electra,
she wasn't pretty but she was mighty tough

She said anything it can happen,
anything ain't all it appears
Dead men sing their song,
weak men become strong
Pretty women just fly through the air

Chorus

St. Louis County Fair
St. Louis County Fair
Dead men sing their song,
weak men become strong
Pretty women just fly through the air

It was midnight when I laid eyes upon her,
she was walking down fireworks row
She grabbed me like I knew her forever
as the sky was about to explode

We rolled nickels and we ate cotton candy,
took a ride on the old ferris wheel
And we kissed by the lights of the city
at the top we hung by our heels

Won a black cat at the ring toss,
shot plastic ducks in a pond
Well the first time I kissed her,
I started to miss her
And just in a flash she was gone

Repeat Chorus

I walked further up the midway,
a barker yelled come on inside
For 10 tickets I will introduce you to a loved one
That was too soon to die

Now who in the world would believe it,
I almost started to cry
There was my Grandma and Grandpa
smiling sweetly, dancing side by side

Young love that never got older,
old love that always stayed young
Old love or new love,
false love or true love,
It just keeps you hanging on

Repeat Chorus

The next day I went to the fairground
where the carnival lights used to be
You know I might have been dreaming
all I saw was a hobo sleeping under a tree

Then the Junkboy rolled out of the bushes with a
martini wedding ring in his ear
Had a postcard from Lady Samantha
said see you sailors same time next year

True love it never comes easy,
true love ain't all that it seems
It may last forever, you can never say never
or you're left with a song and your dreams

Repeat Chorus

Words and Music by Paul Metsa

IMAGINARY FLOWERS

I sent you imaginary flowers through a window
carried by a red cardinal with baby blue eyes for
knew you were sleeping

I sent some lilacs too with their scent that turns sleep to
dreams Remember that dream, the one by the fountain,
Central Park, or was it Mexico?

Everyone was dancing, and one couple danced
        closer than the rest
Near the shadows where the music circled them in a
        Corner
One man, I think it was me, saw you amidst the
        colors of the crowd
the same colors of these flowers, imaginary flowers
next to you when you wake up
Lots of blue flowers, one red one like a dress
and faded yellow that finds its color as the sun rises
        again
as it always does
I waved at you
but really wanted to blow you a kiss instead

GODS AND MONKEYS

And in this night
with only the moon and a mountain or two
between us

If you believe in God or monkeys
or anything in between
(and everything is in between, we know that don't we?)

And in this night
Eva Cassidy shouts and sings
and whispers in golden cloud glow
in an almost-painted kitchen by Bruce
a handyman and everyman

And all these words I write
stripping layers from every shadow
I tried to forget but can't
because that is how language works
as does truth

My guitar, my oldest and dearest friend
beckons me from that dusty corner
in that almost-painted kitchen

May I be strong enough to hold her tight
Like I did you and still will
And hold my arms out, a door that never closes

But is now almost painted a golden tan, matching and table
Like your skin, and hair, and heart
All of that
And everything that matches
And always will

THE MISSISSIPPI RIVER LIKE THE BERLIN WALL

I have played close to 5,000 gigs in Minneapolis since 1978 and less than 50 in St. Paul. I did do a week residency at a club in Novosibirsk, Siberia, in 1999, which happens to be the Sister City of St. Paul, which has to count for something. The Mississippi River, for this Minneapolis musician, has seemed like the Berlin Wall, which one would only cross under the cover of night to play.

My band *Cats Under the Stars* (a tad bi-polar as we were either a jazz trio in tuxedos or a five-piece rock band in blue jeans, depending on the gig) were introduced to the Capital City in the early 1980s, where we first played O'Connell's on the east end of Grand Avenue, a longstanding old-school swanky supper club that featured yellow vinyl booths, killer martinis, steaks fit for Texas cattlemen, and where the house musician that booked us would, for some reason, adorn the back of the stage with an unlikely and large Confederate flag on the nights he played. (On his off nights, he ran an illegal gambling house in Afton). Farther west on Grand, a Sunday night stint at McCafferty's Pub — a touch of Dublin, as it were, where we were introduced to the magic and wonder of the Macalester female student population and Guinness.

Other gigs included Ryan's Corner, a bar swathed in stale beer and cigarette smoke in the no man's land that was Lowertown, wedged in between weekly appearances by young bands who worshiped at the altar of Ozzy Osbourne. There was a gig at Webbes, a short-lived club near Harriet Island, where the owner (who thought he was getting the jazz trio) was horrified after the rock band showed up and finished the night standing atop our amplifiers. We were fired before the last drink was poured. We also graced the stage at the Buttery in downtown St. Paul, a cool little jazz joint and one of the few that kept its doors open after they rolled up the rest of the streets at dusk.

The Cats broke up in 1984, but not before we had climbed the ladder high enough to not only make an appearance on the Prairie Home Companion radio show, but also to get invited to the Keillor family apartment (across the alley from O'Connell's) after the show for a perfectly St. Paul evening of Pictionary and a holiday trumpet solo from young Jason Keillor. I vividly remember Garrison winning the game with an answer that had his name all over it... "The Magnificent Ambersons!"

I put out my first LP, *Paper Tiger*s, in 1984, and the newly formed Paul Metsa Group found itself, every now and then, back east of the Mississippi River. We found fans at both Macalester and the University of St. Thomas and were invited to play Spring Bashes at both schools. Not much later, I would be invited to proudly play several benefits and protests on the steps of the State Capitol, often being able to enjoy the view looking down the hill as the lights of downtown begin their slow burn, releasing the ghosts that freely roam between the Commodore and St. Paul Hotel. Norm Coleman invited me to play his first fundraiser while he announced his run for Mayor at O'Gara's Bar, and I was honored when he also asked me to play his Mayoral Inaugural. I recently played the Humphrey-Mondale Dinner (featuring Hillary Clinton and Bernie Sanders) at the St. Paul River Centre and performed the National Anthem with my buddy and superb soul singer Willie Walker, a 50-year resident of East St. Paul. It was a good night, followed by a soulful late-night breakfast of Potatoes O'Brien at Mickey's Diner.

As I was packing up my gear on Kellogg Avenue after the soiree, I recalled many of these gigs, and my musical roots in St. Paul. While braving the cold of blasts off the river, I remembered one other gig. It was the neighborhood Irish joint called the Half Time Rec. We met a fellow there that night who offered to be our soundman. He owned a sound system and had a truck to transport his and our gear. We hired him on the spot. A few months later we found out he was also a cocaine dealer. Not long after, we realized that he got busted and his truck and our gear were impounded. We had to retrieve our gear, which was now housed in the St. Paul Police Impound Lot. We got our equipment and as we were leaving, the desk sergeant checked the inventory and called to us as we were almost out the door, "Are you guys going to be needing the Triple Beam Scale?"

Cats Under the Stars
Skip Nelimark, John Pasternacki, Tim O'Keefe, and Paul Metsa
(Photo by Rodney Jackson)

HONEYMOON IN DRAG ALLEY

Honeymoon in Drag Alley
watch how you get your kicks
For your lover's secret handshake
might be the high five of a witch
You think you found your true
love 'til you realize the switch

it's just Drag Alley's bag of tricks
it's just Drag Alley's bag of tricks

The last saint in Drag Alley
is walkin' on the wire
Even church mice change denominations
fallen angels are for hire
You thought love would last forever
run out of gas and blew a tire
Sang the hellcat in the choir
sang the hellcat in the choir

<u>Chorus</u>

Love is gonna come around
first goes up and then goes down
Love is like a ferris wheel
goes round and round, how does it feel
Love is like a hurricane
blows through town brings drivin' drain
drivin' rain, drivin' rain

They come from sunburnt cities
and they're tryin' to get rich
For every hero's handshake
there will be a pilgrim in the ditch
And the hangman in Drag Alley
might be the doorman at the Ritz
It's just Drag Alley's bag of tricks
It's just Drag Alley's bag of tricks
It's just Drag Alley's bag of tricks

Words and Music by Paul Metsa

HUBERT SUMLIN

Sitting on Top of the World

◆ *A Tribute* ◆

"That's what I'm talkin' about!"

Hubert Sumlin was one of America's most influential guitarists and one of the nicest men I have ever met. As the lead guitarist for blues king Howlin' Wolf, he put his signature fluid and sinewy guitar stamp on most of Wolf's greatest hits, including "*Spoonful*," "*Wang Dang Doodle*," and "*Smokestack Lightnin'*," among others. They shared an almost telepathic musical relationship, best described by Hubert as "I was him, and he was me." He was revered by guitarists such as Jimi Hendrix, Jimmy Page, Stevie Ray Vaughn, and Jeff Beck, and was named by *Rolling Stone* magazine as the 43rd greatest guitar player of all time. Though I have only met a few of the other 100, I am sure Hubert was the nicest of the bunch.

I got a chance to get to know Hubert when I was booking Famous Dave's Barbeque and Blues Club in Minneapolis in 2002. Curt Obeda, a great Minneapolis blues guitarist and musician, was a friend of Hubert's and put me in touch with his agent. I booked him four times over the years (he'd always be backed up by Obeda's superb group The Butanes). Over the years he played the club, we became good friends and I always looked forward to his visits to Minneapolis.

I will never forget the first time I picked him up at the airport. It was an early morning flight, a time most musicians haven't even gotten out of bed. I met him at the luggage carousel at 7 a.m. He was dressed in a neatly pressed three-piece grey suit wearing a colorful tie that was a gift from Bob Dylan. He had several shiny pieces of lapel jewelry and was wearing a sharp businessman's

Stetson hat. I shook his hand and was enchanted by his eyes that could only be described as Icelandic blue. He traveled light, carrying only a guitar in a leather gig bag and a small duffel bag of clothes.

I felt like I had met my new best friend, which is how I am sure everyone else felt when meeting him for the first time.

I had my cassette tape recorder along and taped our entire conversation on the car ride to the hotel. His gentle voice and style of speaking were both delightfully musical, punctuated by laughs, an electric smile, and when he agreed with what you were saying, replied, "That's what I'm talkin' about!" He had a certain buoyant childlike innocence that Obeda and I later agreed reminded us of Peter Sellers' character Chauncey Gardner in the movie *Being There*. He was a very special man and truly one of a kind.

It was the week before Christmas and Hubert told me he was invited to spend Christmas with Keith Richards and his family. He then told me an amazing story about how the last time he visited, Keith met him at the door of his estate and did back flips through the kitchen and living room while welcoming Hubert into his home. Hubert punctuated this flabbergasting image and story by saying, "That guy is Super!" Mind-blowing stuff and funny as hell. When he took the stage that evening, he'd raise both hands like Haile Selassie and the crowd would rise to cheer him. Like I said, he made everybody feel like he was their best friend.

During one of his gigs in town, I asked him about his legendary 1955 Gibson Gold Top Les Paul, the guitar that he used on many of those Howlin' Wolf tracks and that sat atop those tunes like a rattle on a desert snake. He then proceeded to tell me a story that many of us probably had never heard. He was on a tour of Europe in 1964 with a cavalcade of American blues artists, including Chicago blues guitarist Homesick James. At one of the outdoor gigs, the wind kicked up and it started to rain, destroying Homesick James' guitar. When Homesick was telling Hubert what happened, he started to cry, as it was his only guitar. Without thinking twice, Hubert gave him that '55 Les Paul. Think about that for a minute and marvel at the essence of the man.

I always looked forward to picking up Hubert at the airport and, if we had time, taking him out for lunch. I'd take him to Nye's Polonaise Room, and he loved the broiled walleye. Once, after lunch, we stopped by my house so he could meet my dog Blackie. Hubert was a dog lover, like me, and missed his dog at home. Blackie, who didn't cotton to just anyone, completely hit it off with him, letting him gently pet him while Hubert lit up like a Christmas tree. Two kindred souls, indeed.

Hubert then asked me to grab my guitar and, in a moment embedded in my memory like it was yesterday, showed me the lick he created for "*Smokestack Lightnin'*," one of the greatest blues songs ever recorded. I could have died and gone to Heaven. He then recorded the outgoing message on my phone machine, flabbergasting every blues fan that ever called my house. "Hi. This is Hubert Sumlin. PLEASE leave a message for Paul Metsa." You could hear the smile in his voice. And if that wasn't enough, he always made a point of catching my Happy Hour set before his show, and one night told me he put a mojo blessing on my guitar when I wasn't looking. I couldn't have been more honored or touched. I wouldn't sell that guitar for a million dollars.

There was never a time with Hubert that didn't have moments of pure gold. He loved to tell the story that he snuck out as a young teenager to hear Howlin' Wolf at a local juke joint in Mississippi, and too young to get in, fell through a skylight into Wolf's lap. How Wolf sent for him from Mississippi to Chicago to play with him, then fired him and sent him back home to learn to play without a pick. He did, and upon returning to Chicago, they made history together. He told me his first wife's name was Evelyn, and I told him that was my grandmother's name, which I thought was a sweet coincidence. He paused and said, "She tried to poison me." It doesn't get any more bluesy than that.

The last time I saw and heard Hubert was in March 2011, at Orchestra Hall in Minneapolis (he passed on 12/4/11). It was a Tribute to Robert Johnson and included David "Honeyboy" Edwards (who was with Robert Johnson the night he was poisoned and then died), who passed away last year as well. Hubert strolled out to the stage pulling his oxygen tank behind him and gave the crowd a one-armed Haile Selassie wave as the crowd stood to meet him. Without hesitation, he broke into Howlin' Wolf's version of "*Sitting on Top of the World,*" and you could tell by his smile and his playing that he was. (Damn you, Hubert. You sure know how to make a grown man cry!) I went backstage, hugged him, saying both hello and goodbye, as we both knew it might be our last time seeing each other.

I had a dream about Hubert the other night. I was flying at about 100 mph, ten feet above the ground, on my way over a busy interstate highway to go and see Hubert box Keith Richards at Madison Square Garden. That is a crazy dream for sure, made even crazier by the image of Keith Richards wearing boxing trunks, boxing gloves, and shirtless. Keith came out first, and then Hubert, dressed in a three-piece gold suit. The dream ended there, though my money would have been on Hubert.

My gal Amy and I were awakened by her rooster, King Richard, crowing his nine chickens out of their slumber. I reached over to pet Blackie, who always slept next to us on a blanket. He stood slowly and cocked his head sideways, and I could only wonder if he didn't dream this dream as well.

Hometownfocus.us, July 13, 2012

Paul Metsa and Hubert Sumlin
(Photo by Rich Benson)

NO MONEY DOWN

The first time you told me I was on the wrong side of Jesus
The second time you told me from a window
on the dark side of town
The third time you told money does just what it pleases
You can wish for the world if you want it for no money down

Sisters of sorrow walk by in the company of strangers
Strangers in shadows walk by screaming barely a sound
They put their faith in the future even when they don't
want to
They can wish for the world when they want to for no
money down

Chorus

No money down, No money down
You can walk like that, you can talk like that
You can wish for the world if you want to for no money down

Rag man walk by rusted by invisible raindrops
Pearls and those diamonds on the necks of the debutante's gown
The hangman's backstage while the curtain is rising
It is opening night get a ticket for no money down

There's a room at the poorhouse just grab a number
There's a room at the White House, just stand in line
There's a room at the Penthouse with a ledge by the window
A wish for the world if you want it for no money down

There's a gate up in Heaven that will open if you get lucky
There's a doorway in Hell that will close if you fall down
There's a ring in the circus in the meantime all options open
You can wish for the world if you want it for no money down

Repeat Chorus

Words and Music by Paul Metsa

FROGS

And when frogs barked at midnight
Like blues singers yet to be born
Nothing more than a whistle through a
rusted throat

or maybe thousands of them
But who is counting?
Not a lonely bluebird
Who is first there in spring
Or no, some graying and golden owl
that has been there all along

Nor an eagle that could fly with one broken wing
Or a lesser bird, that couldn't fly with two
All bird whistles, and songs from other animals
that hide in broke down branches and trees
and hold beak to beak, or a hand reaching out to
broken branch from a broken limb
Dylan said, everything is broken

But I must disagree
Limbs both break and disappear and
hearts from water become great things

And dust, then gold, then gods that walk among us
And song
Forever there
Like it has always been

HEY, DAD

(Midnight Note from Blackie)

Remember the day we met?
You and Renea, looking for a dog
One that just came up to your knee
At Contented Critters, the animal rescue place that
wouldn't kill any of us—
I was sent there from another shelter where I would have
ended up on Doggie Death Row
As they said I was a total head case

A 900-lb. pig, a three-legged horse, a blind turtle, dozens
of critters of things with tails and four legs, and
stray cats — lots and lots of cats,
You'd later refer to it as Dr. Doolittle on LSD
'Cause you wanted to replace the healing energy
That saved your father from death's door

And you had spent six weeks, 2-3-4 days a week
Driving up to visit him at St. Mary's Hospital in Duluth
After he fell down a flight of stairs, breaking three ribs
and puncturing a lung
Not worrying about losing your job
More worried about losing your dad

And he, in a coma, wrists and arms swollen
As the booze was trying to leave his veins
And you hoped to God he wouldn't die
Because you could never forgive him
For ending his last chapter like this
Gambling daily, at the bar, brandy-stained pull tabs,
up to his knee

On Chestnut Street, where he grew up above The
Roosevelt Bar
As an only child with loving parents
And how proud they would have been to see him
Served two terms as Mayor, and become one of the
best dressed men in town

His dad Emil owned the bar, and mother Elna ran a
rooming house above it
Emil would cash the checks of lumberjacks, holding
enough money back
So the lumberjacks could take the rest home to their
families
After several days of rewarding themselves for those 16-
hour days
Of cutting down birch and pine trees in sometimes 30
below weather
Elna would wash clothes and feed those in the 16-room
Hotel
Including "Steve the Russian" who took a shine to you
And bought you cheese popcorn and soda pop in the bar
When you visited Grandma and Grandpa
And after selling the bar moved across Chestnut Street
To a small three-room apartment above another bar
Where on sleepovers, you'd fall asleep to the blinking neon
lights on the street below
Grandma would feed the stray cats on the alley porch
The best fed alley cats in town, some becoming the size of small
mountain lions
And you will always remember when you drove Grandpa
down
To the hospital in Minneapolis, he with cancer, and you both
in Grandma's '68 dark green Dodge Polara

And as you drove away, Grandma looked at both of you, in a
plaid skirt from another time,
Feeding the cats, then cried, that memory like it was
yesterday

And your father went on to marry a Princess
After meeting her on a blind date in Duluth
Born in the shadow of the statue of *Paul Bunyan and the
Blue Ox* in Bemidji, Minnesota
And her relationship with her own father was such
That she took a room in a graveyard hotel while in high
school
And sang in the high school choir, and had the voice of
an angel

She became a nurse, and how she might have
Cared for your dad from Heaven, as she passed 8 years
before
And you read newspapers, and magazines while visiting
dad
Paying special attention to the ads from local humane
shelters

with pictures of homeless doggies and kitties like me
While you combed Dad's hair, and wiped his brow
And cut his nails on his perfect typewriter hands
And pasted bits of papers on hospital room ceiling that
said
Sisu, the word for God within us all
That actually meant, determination beyond all reason
Which is what he taught you, John, Jackie, and Kathy
And during that time, you, had to remove his wedding
ring,
a Las Vegas lucky seven pinkie ring for good luck, and a
gold

wrist bracelet, to keep the pressure off his hands so his
wrists didn't explode

And while reading the humane shelter ads, you made a
promise to the Universe
That if dad recovers, you will adopt a dog (one that came
up to your knee)
To transfer the healing energy that saved your dad
And recover he did, and this is where I come in
So, you and Renea show up at Contented Critters in
Makinen, Minnesota
You perused the 35 or so dogs there, mostly larger hunting
dogs abandoned by hunters
When they got too old to hunt (btw, fuck those guys)
You didn't really see any dogs that would work as they
were all too big

And asked Renea to get your checkbook to leave a
donation
And then, as you were leaving, I barked
Barked loudly, in fact, louder than I've ever barked
And you asked Walt, caretaker of all of us, "Who the hell
is that?"
And he said "Blackie…but he has issues…"
(Well, who, the good goddamn, doesn't?)
Of course, I did, taken as a pup from a deadly shelter,
then to Contented Critters
Where a farm family adopted me immediately (as you
noticed right off the bat, I am one good lookin' SOB!)
That kept me on a damn leash 24-7, and fed me when
they remembered

So, of course, I chewed through the leash

And ran like hell into the frozen woods for a damn year,
amidst the balsam and the pine
And I chewed grass when the snow melted, broke my
tooth on a rock.
And when the snow melted and the ice disappeared
from the rivers, I then drank that

And I shit under pine trees, behind rocks, and far enough
away
So the goddamn wolves, and whatever else, would
never smell me
Or find me, and I left, as I still do, the rest of the animals
alone

And I remember when my bark brought you to my cell-
hell hole-cage
You were ready to leave, I knew you were
And my eyes burst forth like German submarines
eyeing the American Merchant Marine
And my ears pinned back, like some pit bull from hell
'Cause I had to
And Renea opened the cage and I walked out
And she said, "You don't look so tough!"
And I wasn't really, just determined, and sat on my
haunches, right ear up, left ear down
Like you tell the story, like the Flying Nun
So, for $65 I was yours, to be picked up in two weeks
And then you got me, and got your dad as well

He to a hospital in Northern Minnesota, you walking
him out of the hospital
At 6 feet tall, and 103 pounds, and not able to write his
name, walk, or talk
And as you took him, in a van from Northern
Transportation

Your Dad turned gray, and about to pass out, you saw
It was the time to turn on the oxygen
Which the farewell nurse forgot to do
The little things these nurses forget to do, your mother being one
Just about the time they stopped wearing their 3-pointed hats

With pins, and bright white uniforms, Napoleon would approve
And he got home to Cook, and so did I, to the warmth of your Nordeast home
Your dad would continue his recovery at a half nursing home-half hospital
And you left me with Renea to go visit dad, all by my doggie lonesome
After her brother, who was living with her, came home from work, I saw an opening,and ran out of the house
And now I was lost in your urban jungle in south Minneapolis
For three long days and three cold nights, before I was hit by one, maybe two cars
At 44th and Chicago, one hell of a busy intersection

And one big black angel, walking his tiny dog, slowly scraped me to the side of that street
And held me, and called Animal Rescue
And then they came, and they called you too.
And you cried, never being able to excuse yourself
If I never came back
But crying, I think perhaps a tear or two of joy

And there I was at the Golden Valley Emergency Vets
Golden Valley, which Steinbeck said in *Travels with Charley*
"Is neither Golden nor a valley"
And there I was
They took me out on a colorless blanket
Knocked out like Sonny Liston, but breathing like a baby child

And the doctor said, give me your credit card, and call me in the morning

And you did, and came to see me, now in an oxygen tank
Fat lip, busted back end, and all
And I saw you, and Renea, and though we had only Known each other for a couple of weeks
I saw my Daddy's eyes, and one ear went up and one went down
You made good on your promise and told the doctor to work his magic
And then remember when I wrote my first Christmas card, a and told the tale
How my magic bark caught your ear, and our innocent souls began to meld
You covered your bedroom in plastic, my blankie and pillow by your bed,
Dragging my ass around, and you took me out every morning to do my business
We'd sit together on the back porch enjoying the autumn morning sunlight
And after a while, oh, how I tried to stand, day after day
And I tried, and tried, and fell on my ass, time and time again
And then, that day, when I wobbled, bucked up, and

finally stood on all fours
That was a glorious day for both of us, wasn't it?
The first time I saw you cry, and I shed a few tears myself
The kind of thing you don't read in the Bible, but probably should

And I did not bark in your house, now my house, until after Christmas Surprising the holy hell out of you

And while you adopted me to transfer the healing energy of your dad's recovery
And instead, I did a canine reenactment of your dad's accident
Well, blame that on the twisted logic and humor of the Universe
Like you humans say, "shit happens."
But your dad and me really bonded as survivors
And now you had yet another story to tell

And that was the beginning of a 16-year glory ride
Your buddy Terry Carlson said I'd light up any room I'd walk into

And that's how I hope I will be remembered
Somebody needs to write that story, and while we are at it
Could I have a few treats?
And that letter ended:

Price of adoption: $65
Price of emergency Vet in Golden Valley: $1,200
Price of UMN Vet Hospital and Intensive Care: $3,600
Price of having MN second best folk singer take me out at 6 a.m. and hold me up while I poop: "Priceless!"

Merry Christmas, your $5,000 alarm clock,
Blackie
P.S. And yes, maybe I picked you.

ATTIC SONG

Gold fades
but not quickly
nor to another color
Like an old dog who turns from black
to gray but retains its love

Throughout the cold rain and snow
like the greatest love should and sometimes does
but if not always holds a door open to the dead
and those that have gone before us

And we'll return, in the ghost skin
of all tomorrow's children
that shines
like salmons breaking water in the sun

And when that sun goes down
shed this skin to next
in the many-colored coat that keeps us warm
in whatever the next day brings

Something we can whistle to
or sing in attics' song
In tune, not that it has to be
In all keys, like God said
When He wasn't looking
and gave us song, skin, and breath
and heartbeat at any speed
Highway of life and death
but life first, and life only

At this candlelit moment among friends,
strangers and those we have yet to know

Breathe slowly
All we have, as we speak
is time
Songs before us
and after

WILLIE MURPHY

Honey from the Bee

♦ *A Tribute* ♦

"Gotta be funky."

All male musicians are Mama's boys and Willie Murphy was no exception. Inspired at the tender age of 3 when at his mother's knee, tears streaming down his face, enchanted by the beauty of her piano playing and singing, the salty seeds were planted on what would become nothing less than a hero's journey. His mother's melody sparked a vision quest that would both lead and sustain him throughout his life, caressing his muse as he wrestled the toxic dual demons of the music business and those of his own making, to eventually emerge bloody, unbowed, and pulsing as the heart and soul of the Minneapolis music scene for over half a century.

Real heroes are in short supply these days, and Murphy always remained one of mine. Whether leading *Willie and the Bumblebees*, his rowdy rhythm and blues posse that could have sprung fully formed from a Sam Peckinpah fever dream – starting soul fires and burning down every dance floor they played, in the process uniting neighbors and strangers in a land of 1,000 moonshine dances – or holding forth at the 400 Bar on Cedar and Riverside, just a barrelhouse piano anchored by his hammer of a left hand, a right foot keeping time like a volcanic metronome, and a voice that could pluck from the cosmos slivers of Little Richard, Howlin' Wolf, Robert Johnson, or Percy Sledge at a moment's notice from invisible shooting stars – often in the same set, sometimes in the same song, but always Willie Murphy – reaching for that midnight rainbow, howling at whatever moon was left.

He started playing bass in high school, often the only white cat in the band, eventually developing a style that resembled legendary Motown bassist James Jamerson in his ability to weave a double dose of rhythm and melody anchoring and propelling the song, often liberating it from what Robert Wyatt called "the tyranny of 4/4 time." Maybe the ghost of Oscar Pettiford, a fellow Minneapolitan and bassist who held down the holy house of the Duke Ellington band from 1945-48 – perhaps a molecule or two of him incarnated into Willie's hands and soul. Either way, it was Willie's bass for me, thundering the Bees' relentless wave after taller wave of tribal rhythmic patterns, a horn section riding and riffing on top, hypnotizing crowds every time I saw them play, often to the point of pure orgasmic frenzy. It was simply impossible not to dance (unless you were in a cadaverous state) and for those that knew Willie, nothing made him happier than a packed, sweaty dance floor. He considered it one of his highest callings, and where his congregation was to be found. And yet it was just one of the things that made this street preacher and music evangelist special.

Memphis-born soul singer extraordinaire Willie Walker, who moved to Minneapolis 50 years ago and is now the most nominated musician in the 40-year history of the Blues Foundation Annual Award Ceremonies, used to front Willie and the Bees in the late '60s (leaving some to wonder which Willie we are talking about). Walker left because, as he told me, "You couldn't make any money with Murphy, as most of the gigs back then were community benefits." In fact, the Bees were referred to as the "people's band." Murphy delighted in it and wore that handle proudly until the very end of his life. He was a stone-cold beatnik-based hippie, an avowed Marxist, and never gave up on the idea of a better world—solidarity through song. The times might have changed, but Willie never did. Never sold out either—his belief system and moral compass anchoring him in the swirling madness and morass of modernity.

His personal and professional lives were no walk in the park. Even after sobering up in the early 1980s (no 30-day treatment for Willie—he saw the light after a weekend in detox), he still suffered severe bouts of depression and insomnia. He'd have several years of steady house gigs, production jobs and showcase gigs, followed by years of falling off people's radar, doing the musician's hustle of waking up with two fingers crossed on one hand and the other not feeling like dialing the phone to face another afternoon of rejection. It was a drill he knew well, yet over the long run, and often in spite of it, he never stopped creating or dreaming. Pause, yes, but never stop. From folk to funk, there was no style of music this side of Igor Stravinsky that he couldn't play. He was a bassist, an acoustic and electric guitarist, a piano pounder, vocalist, composer, arranger, producer, bandleader, soul renegade and philosopher king.

Willie the man was complex, inquisitive, well read, a huge fan of foreign films, a jazz buff, a contrarian, obstinate, and on a good day, a total sweetheart. He was fearless and never backed down or sacrificed his principles. His hair rarely saw a comb or brush, nor his snazzier suit coats, for the cooler gigs, a dry cleaner. He was like Einstein that way – the mad professor constantly tinkering and searching for answers to his various musical equations. While listening to him was also a supreme pleasure in whatever format on any given night, you knew Willie NEVER was going to phone it in—the bandstand as sacred space.

To know Willie Murphy was to have the pleasure of sitting in his living room on a battered couch in front of a coffee table full of Socialist magazines, books of poetry, song lyrics, coffee stains, cigar burns and ashes dotting the room like ancient hieroglyphics. Willie held forth, usually holding a guitar in his lap playing little abstract blues riffs punctuating articulate thought and philosophy, while he smoked his small cigars, reminding one of Mark Twain, if Twain lived in the Inner City in a less-than-perfect neighborhood. You'd always feel you were in the presence of a real artist, one who led his life as if he had no other choice. He didn't.

While listening to Willie over the years was one of the supreme pleasures of my life, working with Willie was not always easy. I had just gotten a well-paying job as a Music Director at a local upscale blues club, brought in to try and turn the club around. I booked a solid lineup of the greatest blues bands in town, including Dave "Snaker" Ray, the Butanes, and Willie Murphy, among others. My first big show was going to be the end of September, 2001. Then 9/11 happened and we turned it into a fundraiser for the NYC firemen who were in town at another event collecting money in rubber fire boots still coated with the sacred dust of bones and falling buildings. Willie was going to kick off the evening at 5 p.m. The man for whom the club was named was there, as were all his friends, and every muckety-muck that worked for the corporation.

The place was packed, anticipation high, and everybody was ready to have a rockin' good time. Willie came up, fiddled around with his piano, adjusted his microphone, only to say loudly and to all in attendance, "They call this a blues club? It's barely a (insert F bomb) restaurant?"

My buddy Dave Ray looked over at me, just before I almost passed out, and said, "That's Murphy…working on his book back!" In retrospect, I wouldn't change a thing, and to a certain degree, he was right.

Willie was a shaman. We didn't go hear Willie to be entertained, we went to be healed, and we always were. He knew how good he was, and so did we. The source of his music was as pure as the driven snow, and at his core, so was he. John Coltrane said the goal of his music was for his audience to "enjoy the capacity of a meaningful life." Willie gave us that in spades.

Willie named his last band the Angel Headed Hipsters, copped from a line in Allen Ginsberg's poem, "Howl."

"...angelheaded hipsters burning for the ancient heavenly connection to the starry dynamo in the machinery of night."

Willie now joins two other West Bank giants—Bill Hinkley and Dave "Snaker Ray"—in both heavenly connection and exile, three kings whose music and memory may well outlast us all.

The last time I saw Willie was in the summer of 2018. I was driving, windows down, along River Road on the south side of the Mississippi River. I looked to my left and there on the upper side of the bank was Willie with his beloved dog Clyde, in a Hawaiian shirt and cut-offs exposing legs whiter than the clouds above. He was kind of jogging in place with quick pixie-like steps—blues Tai chi.

I smiled, slowed down, honked, and waved. He smiled back, looking like he had the world by the bonnet, and I caught a glimpse of the magic in his eyes that twinkled when Willie was on his game.

I thought of him dancing in place, after he passed on Sunday, and again when I woke up today. Like fog lifting from a mirror, there was Willie Murphy—running, jumping, standing still.

MinnPost, January 29, 2019

Willie Murphy and Paul Metsa
(Photo by Rick Marcus)

ROBOTS ON DEATH ROW

You don't like my train,
baby you don't have to drive my track
Tell your switchblade monkey he don't have
to ride your back
Tell your half-moon waitress it ain't no high wire show
You drop old lovers like dominoes,
your barb wired blanket is a ready to go
    Just like a robot on death row

Shoot dogs, train the doctors
Who put the bell on you, airmen in helicopters
You said they fell on you
Your mechanical street queen, you can feel his whistle blow
Ain't no difference mama plugged in Romeo
You're the first to ask questions but the last one to know
    Just like a robot on death row

Your piano is poison they buried your windowsill
You lick your lips for no reason my broke-down whippoorwill
My cast iron princess is now turpentine
I want to ask you about those exploding valentines
You sit in the corner donkeys are wild in Mexico
    Just like a robot on death row

Throw rocks in the river, river gonna run you down
You're an Indian giver you live at the lost and found
I can tell by your shoes that you walk on the water
It ain't no news at all you led the lambs to slaughter
Will you be saved by the soldiers that know?
    Just like a robot on death row

You made me pay for what you gave to the others for free
Your man-boy told me how you got your master's degree
You keep all your goodness in a porcelain dish
You traded forgiveness for a black hooded wish
Your tongue is in traction you can't tell what you know
    Just like a robot on death row

I'll buy you a thumb-ride, give you a broken wheel
There's holes in your raincoat, baby I know how that feels
You wouldn't answer the door if you were knockin' outside
Looked at the eight ball saw floorshow suicide
Your guardian angel packed her bags hit the road
    Just like a robot on death row

Words and Music by Paul Metsa

WALKIN' THE DOG

Helicopters circle sleeping neighborhoods, lone dog walker patient as pup smells every bush and fire hydrant, moon playing pinochle with next door planets, Mars wails like stardust Buddha, waiting for time to tell, though it never does, gravel alleys betray their small stones and bottle cap moments wishing in broken clock time for hooves of bygone horses to walk again upon them with a democratic gait, heads held high and manes softly rustled by forgiving winds.

Catholic church ladies – some in shawls, some not – church organs moan deeply from a secret place – milkmen at the ready – while those church ladies both ready to confess and then replace – young soldiers now just in baby cribs – years later in Fort Bragg or some other place – the world it turns slowly now – and before I rest my case – these images roll 'round my head – I hope for something that comes after them – something golden or at least as meaningful – or at least to at last breakeven – or at least something to take their place.

A NIGHT TO REMEMBER

I spent one of the most amazing (if at times harrowing) nights of my life in 1990 or so with the late greats Guy Clark and Townes Van Zandt. They were in town for a show and happened into the 5 Corners where I had a weekly Tuesday night gig (237 consecutive ones, I might add). They were riding a deep whiskey wave, on a mission from God to find "Spider" John Koerner. I had met them both briefly before and was delighted to tell them that Spider might be bartending across the street at Palmer's Bar. Sure enough, John was there, and when I got off my gig, I walked over for last call. One thing led to another and the four of us found ourselves downtown at the Radisson Hotel with a bottle of whiskey, a few party favors, and our guitars.

About 2 in the morning, they asked John to play a few, and then the guitar started to get passed around – a song each and a pull of whiskey. I'd play a tune of mine about every third go-around and let the masters hold sway. Townes was adamant that there be "no cussing" and after my first tune said, "That ain't nothing but hogwash." Nothing like getting seriously dissed by the Jesus of songwriters. The next time around, summoning courage from the Cutty Sark, I played my tune "Jack Ruby," which I had recently finished. After that, Townes said, "Now that's better, much better."

The night continued to pick up steam. Each song played became a golden link in this beautifully surreal magic chain, and as I stumbled onto Hennepin Avenue to cab it home, I was so amazed by it all, I wondered if it actually happened. It did, and it remains one of my sweetest musical memories. It was what it is all about.

Paul Metsa and "Spider" John Koerner
(Photo by Baby Grant Johnson)

ONWARD THROUGH THE FOG

I drank with Joe Ely, he drank me to the floor
We wrote poems for Jesse Taylor the linebacker of the blues for evermore
Threw Tarot Cards with Jimmie Dale across Jalapeno Charlie's kitchen floor
Helped Butch Hancock carry lumber that built Lubbock or Leave It
With every stolen 2x4 while Jimmy LaFave was singing
Dylan's best some say Senor
The Hole in the Wall my first Austin show
A crowd that listened and a generous pour
With Larry Monroe back at Hut's Diner as
Tex Thomas sang that song about crazy glue
Right before set four
Marcia Ball and Tish Hinojosa inside La Zona Rosa
Danial Johnston outside in black and white
Just like it was before
James White outside of the Broken Spoke
Taking cover at the door
Toni Price down at the bus stop her voice still haunts me
And like eagle's wing did soar
David Grissom buys a gold guitar from
Smilin' Ray at the Heart of Texas store
Ray Benson in boots as big as Texas
Cooly steeped in the swing of Texas lore
Alejandro Escovedo a True Believer
Just like they don't make no more
Michael Priest admires ghost graffiti
As Booka and Edythe plan the nights decor
Margaret Moser in a ponytail keeps all her secrets in a drawer

Townes and Guy they argued and occasionally they swore
Billy Joe Shaver and Stratocaster Eddie stone cold country to the core
Willie rolls yet another one
There's still more smoke rings to explore
Junior Brown at the Continental Sunday nights
Johnny Cash played there in '54
Let's not forget Mr. Evan Johns at the Black Cat Club on 6th Street
Katie bar that H-Bomb door
Sir Doug Sahm with old Sam Houston beneath the Treaty Oak
Skipping stones and smiling by the Colorado river shore
I remember all of it
So God bless Austin, Texas
Forever branded to my core

Stevie Ray Vaughn and Paul Metsa, Austin Music Awards, 1990
(Photo by John Carrico)

MONTY LEE WILKES

◆ *A Tribute* ◆

"Lose the hats."

Monty Lee Wilkes was a scientist, wizard, Northern Minnesota boy, and one of the finest live sound technicians in the world. Born in 1961 in Kettle River, Minnesota, Monty attended a Grateful Dead concert in Madison, Wisconsin, in 1973 with his dad Howie, and became enchanted with the mechanizations of men working the soundboard, as well as the legendary Wall of Sound, the 70-ton sound system the Dead carried with them (along with a lesser amount of drugs). Driving home that night toward the Northern Star, Monty's course and mission in life was set.

He started mixing *MilkBone*, dad Howie's band, at their weekend gigs in St. Louis County roadside taverns before hooking up with Cloquet's gangster-clad rockers, Bugsy Malone. Bugsy and the boys, in a shot at the big time, had a chance to open for Duluth's the Bronx Zoo, who were the toast of the Zenith City at the time.

Monty moved to Duluth and worked not only with the 'Zoo, but started doing sound at places like the Cove Bar in Superior, and the Norshor Theater, among others. Moving up the ladder, the 'Zoo opened for Minneapolis bands like the Suburbs, the Flamin' Oh's, and Johnny Rey and the Reaction. While being encouraged by all the Minneapolis rockers to move to the Twin Cities, it was finally Johnny Rey who offered Monty a job. Off he went, Southbound on Highway 35-W, following his heart, chasing his dream, the wind through the open window in his van having its way with his below-shoulder, Samson-like wavy locks. Like Kris Kristofferson said, "Freedom's just another word, for nothing left to lose."

Monty's reputation preceded him and soon he found himself mixing dozens of bands and working a steady gig at First Avenue – then and now, the greatest rock club in the world. Don't believe me? Ask Prince. As Monty's burgeoning legend grew, he was tapped by Peter Jesperson, manager of the Replacements, to go on the road with the 'Mats, work sound, drive the van, and occasionally babysit this most irascible and fascinating band, considered by many to have been the best band in America at the time.

While many of these tales are told by Monty in Bob Mehr's excellent biography of the band, *Trouble Boys: The True Story of the Replacements*, I had the privilege of hearing Monty tell the tale of how the band piece-by-piece disassembled the van, ripping the cupboards off the wall, covering it and themselves in white paint, until Peter and he had to return the shell of the RV to the rental outfit in Elk River, when one of them said to the agent, who was about to pass out, "Well, we did fill the tank!"

During the amazing telling of this tale in his Northside submarine studio, Monty and I, rolling on the floor in stitches and struggling to catch our breath, both had ice cream headaches at the absolute 'turn-it-up-to-11' absurdity of it all. The man could tell a story. And like he told a friend years later, "You want to know fear? I had to take the Replacements to Graceland!" Monty, truth be told, was fearless.

Monty went from the 'Mats to working sound and road managing a young band out of Olympia, Washington, called Nirvana, who were starting to scream into the stratosphere with their record *Nevermind.* Over the next few years, he worked with a variety of famous independent rock bands, including *The DB's*, *the Smithereens*, *Alice in Chains*, and the *B-52s.* He got into the big money, working with modern country acts like *Carrie Underwood* (or how he put it, "blondes with big breasts"), before he landed in the pilot's seat as the FOH (front-of-house) soundman for Britney Spears—sound board wizard for her shows in stadiums with 80,000 fans in places like Sao Paulo, Brazil. He was as far away from Kettle River as one could get. He had hit the Big Time.

After years of that, he ended up back in Minneapolis, where we met sometime around 2010. With our Northern Minnesota roots, a shared loved of true American Patriotism, and senses of humor forged in the unforgiving fires of the music biz, we bonded immediately. We spent many an afternoon and evening together before he finally let on he had mixed sound for my first big show under my own name, opening for Taj Mahal at the Norshor Theater in Duluth, Minnesota, in 1984. Monty, now still slender, and with greying hair now at Peter Tork's length. I checked out his Facebook page, and sure enough, I remembered him, though back then he had dark curly hair reaching to his belt. Yes, now I remembered him. Monty fucking Wilkes.

We became thick as thieves, and for the next several years, our friendship blossomed like hothouse flowers. Monty had given up drinking years before, replacing his dozen White Russians a night with an equal amount of righteous weed, waking and baking daily, that would give Bob Marley a run for his money.

I was on the board of directors for a group that controlled the Fitgers Brewhouse, one of the first brew pubs in Minnesota, and several other restaurants. I'd drive up to Duluth once a month, and Monty, who loved Duluth as much as I, would tag along and visit his old haunts while I tended to business. On one trip, I made an appointment to meet the Mayor of Duluth to pitch him on an idea I had to create a week-long series of events honoring hometown hero Bob Dylan during his birthday week. Monty was hitting on his pot pipe the whole way up, and I abstained to keep my head clear for the meeting. We got there early. I was a little nervous meeting the mayor, and managed at first to spill my bottle of water all over the visitors' couch. The mayor showed up, and as I was going to shake his hand, I managed to spill my coffee on his secretary's desk, she a sweet older Asian lady who looked at us with a cautious eye. The mayor helped me clean up the coffee and invited us into his office for the meeting, which went well. As we were leaving, the secretary looked at us (Monty never took off his Ray Ban sunglasses) and asked, "Are you gentlemen in the entertainment industry?" Totally busted.

Another time, we were both invited to be judges at the Battle of the Bands at the Duluth Arena. Monty took it very seriously, taking copious notes, one which included to one of the bands, "Lose the hats!" Tough love, as they say.

Monty was diagnosed with lung cancer in 2017. I'd visit him at the Hennepin County Medical Center, always bringing a large pepperoni pizza from his favorite, Carbone's Pizza. The cancer eventually spread to his brain. Trooper that he was, the last big gig he mixed sound for was his hero Curtiss A's Tribute to John Lennon at First Avenue, a show that Curt did every year since the night John Lennon was killed. The place was packed and Monty, in a black leather jacket and fur hat, mixed the group of 16 musicians, strings, two drummers and more in a way that recalled Phil Ramone. If you were lucky enough, you got to stand next to Monty and sound board behind velvet ropes, the VIP section for the most important of VIP's.

In the last week of Monty's life, I reached out to Nate Kranz, one of the majordomos at First Avenue, and suggested that Monty deserved his own star painted on the outside walls of First Avenue, joining the Who's Who of damn near every important rock band of the last 40 years that had played there. He enlisted ace photographer Dan Corrigan, who climbed a ladder and hand-painted Monty's name. I had a gig in Duluth on that Friday, and on the way up, I stopped by to see Monty in Barnum to tell him the news. He was living with his mom and dad, Sandy and Howie (no son ever loved his parents more). He was gaunt, nearly bald, wearing both a face mask and a Johnny Rey and the Reaction T-shirt - the band that brought him to Minneapolis to start his amazing journey.

I held his hand and told him the news. He smiled and said, "Now I can die in peace." We both laughed, knowing that wasn't the point, although one week later he did.

Monty Wilkes and Paul Metsa
(Photo by Cray McCally)

LITTLE BIRDIE

A little birdie told me and then a squirrel
The adopted German Shepherd next door that cries
like a baby girl
until I throw her a dry bone across the chain link fence
after I feed Blackie, the King of all wild dogs
and they remember me as I remember them
Orphans, all of us a long, long way from home
Our spirit in common and as strong as the wind
that blows from all directions
Poetry, both barked and recited
at public libraries and in back yards
where all dogs and poets
are safe and sound and productive
by the midnight fire pit fury of flames
that both warm and protect us
and lets us both, barking or reciting
in carnival shouts or shadow of whispers
go out to and back from the universe
to all from whence we came

AUTOMATIC HEROES

Three key Willie in a coast guard hat flirtin' with the
angel in the Laundromat
She cannot be a day over sixteen

On the box she's got the hip and hop, she dances all night she
never stops
Blows kisses but she don't promise him anything

Willie does the hucklebuck on the back of his old pick-up
Truck
Drives right behind the city marching band

Sings to her from her patio, says he'll be her backyard
Daddio
Falls in the gladiolas and the dogs begin to bark

Chorus

Up in the window, tie up the sheets and come on down
Jump in your feather pillow, be an automatic hero in the
tumblin' town

He loves that black eyed hurricane sittin' pretty in her
baby blue mustang
Sundown cakewalk princess of the strip

Gives her Spanish daisies for her hair, tells her about
Victor the wrestling bear
How he rode the gravy train from Miami his hometown

She's the midnight hit at the school dance, puts Willie in
an all-night trance
Does the hully-gully, the cha-cha, and the frug

Lady fingers blow in Chinatown, ballerinas at the speed
of sound
But all Willie hears is jangling wedding bells

Repeat Chorus

Weepin' willows sway near Golden Gate and Willie ain't
got no time to wait
Asks her if she will be his gypsy queen

Hired a one-way hypnotist, stole a speech from a blind
ventriloquist
But somehow, I think Willie missed his mark

She said it's just like crumbs to a sparrow, you shoot at
me with broken arrows
Why don't you take the bus to outer space?

Well, it hit him like a wrecking ball, and he sells
chimpanzees in St. Paul
You know sometimes things aren't too good on Monkey Island

Repeat Chorus

Words and Music by Paul Metsa
Paul Metsa Music – 1988 – BMI ©

FROM RUSSIA WITH LOVE (A SONGWRITER'S STORY)

Three years ago, I was hired to play at a nightclub in Siberia. I arrived at the Minneapolis–St. Paul International Airport with a guitar, my suitcase, and a 70-pound duffel bag filled with gifts from an American grandmother to Russian granddaughters. I bullied these through security, customs, two five-hour layovers, countless time zones, and at least two languages, one of which I did not speak.

On my final flight from Moscow to Novosibirsk, I was dog tired but too overwhelmed by the experience to sleep. There happened to be only one other passenger still up at that ungodly hour. He was a Russian gentleman who appeared to be around 70, dressed in what could only be called peasant clothes, bopping his bald head wildly to modern headphones.

The seat next to him was empty. I sat down and he offered me a pull off what seemed to be moonshine in an unlabeled bottle. After trying small talk, I realized all we had was insomnia in common, but no common language. He looked like my grandfather, but was dancing in his seat like a teenager. I was filled with trepidation about playing for a foreign audience in a country I grew up fearing, and flush with fatigue.

After a few more pulls off the bottle, he offered me his headphones. Like a huge light at the end of a dark psychic tunnel, I put on the headphones and was stunned to hear America's favorite baritone sing, "I shot a man in Reno just to watch him die." Johnny Cash as universal language.

I shook his hand, smiled, returned the headphones and fell soundly to sleep. Berlin Wall be damned.

Letter to the editor, No Depression
December 2002

MIST

Tomorrow's teardrops
who is to know?
Invisible rain falls on everyone
at points in time
faster than Japanese trains

Wind covers us and asks nothing in return
like yours or mine
a perfect friend
deep in shadow
never seen by the naked eye
yet always there

LETTER TO A FRIEND

Dearest Syd,

What a wonderful world – to remember you on the stairway almost ten years and a song or two later – it seems like yesterday – as good memories should and do – and art like love endures – and words are supposed to do – not unlike Kerouac, you live it as you love it and it seems to love you back, as well it should – letters never written and the words never spoken in the days in between – old Irish memories over a glass of rye and a loud jukebox in a tavern's foreign place, where kisses collide with the real world, where even nighthawks have long since gone asleep – a gutter harmonica plays itself and the ghosts of landlocked airmen sway in unison to a breeze that never blows – empty trumpets blow farewell to lovers never seen – love like that three-legged dog – it just keeps coming back with no newspaper between its teeth and warm breath on master's cheek – broken windowpanes where somebody sometime looked out and dreamt of somewhere else – where Juliet cried 'Where art thou?' but Romeo, long since underground, could only whisper his reply – just another rose in a bleeding hand – blood like mercury, like wasted gold dust daylight drips with the promise of a polyester rag sheep of someone I once knew in this place so long ago – but time is like that – a whore, no doubt – but we knew that – and perhaps that is all we need to know – there is romance in a Texas wind, heart like a tumbleweed – a Cadillac fancy to the good catholic girls – into a pure heart the cowboy comes – into the sunset of someone's sunrise – and hit the trail and don't look back, for all you'll see is shadows and remember that they lie – and you can lie to them but it will get you nowhere and what is satisfaction but to lack the need to have it — when kids not cops wrote with chalk on cement – and maybe that place visits us when our eyes are closed and our dreams like bad television haunt us into not believing it – but you hear it in the occasional train whistle – or when a waitress swears or when a loud guitar slices through this gin joint with the righteous fury that makes poor men proud – and don't forget the tremolo – there is something else at work here, don't even need to know – it is that time when time returns, and I had that time tonight and that was before you asked me about my mother and the color of her eyes – it is something she would have asked someone else – they were hazel, the same color as mine, and when I looked into them, I could see everything that was good and righteous in this world.

I sent this letter to my friend Syd Straw following a performance of hers in Minneapolis a week after my mother's death in May 1994.

JEANNE PETERSON

◆ *A Tribute* ◆

"Age is just a number, but mine is unlisted."

Jeanne Peterson was as fine a Minnesotan as our state ever needs to be remembered for. She was a master musician who plied her trade as a teenager in the smoky jazz clubs of Hennepin Avenue in the 1930s, her voice broadcast between the hog reports on WCCO Radio in the '40s, performances at Met Stadium in the '50s and '60s (including a stint as the Minnesota Twins organist, taking over from her husband, Willard, who died on opening day in '69), to gigs at Dayton's Department Store, almost every cool downtown Twin Cities hotel with a piano, to the majestic Guthrie Theater and most points in between. Her career, in a way, was the musical version of *Lost Twin Cities*.

And true to form, she outlasted almost all of them.

In the wake of her recent passing, her name must now be added to the top of the list of legendary Minnesotans, including Charles Lindbergh, Roy Wilkins, Hugo Black, Judy Garland, Hubert Humphrey, Nellie Stone Johnson, and others. As an artist, her lifelong achievements nestle comfortably with Minnesota talents such as Meridel Le Sueur, Gordon Parks, and Charles Schulz. As a musician first, but next, perhaps the greatest mother this state has ever produced.

Her five kids are all successful professional musicians. You'd think the laws of probability would determine that at least one of them would end up selling insurance, working construction, or maybe even practicing law, if not having a brush with it.

Nope, not the Peterson clan. Mostly self-taught and tutored by Jeanne, they have performed with a Who's Who of American musicians: Bob Dylan, Miles Davis, Leo Kottke, Steve Miller, The Time, Stevie Nicks, David Sanborn, Michael Bolton, the Osmond

Family, and dozens more. Literally and figuratively, Jeanne's legacy extends from Paul Whiteman to Prince and has covered the waterfront. Do I need to add that she raised these kids during their formative years as a single mother?

For Jeanne, raising a family and playing music were all in a day's work. In 2007, a friend asked if I could find a piano player to perform at his wedding reception. I wanted to get him the best in town, so I called Jeanne. She thanked me for calling her but said, "I'd love to, but I have three gigs that day." She was 85 years old.

I saw her for the last time at her 90th birthday celebration at the Old Log Theater in 2012. She looked gorgeous, carried herself with the élan of Jackie Onassis, and was surrounded by her talented brood and other musicians, all cousins celebrating the matriarch of this most talented of bloodlines. She swung like Count Basie and played solos that sounded like Dave Brubeck, punctuated by the raising of her right hand off the keyboard à la Liberace after she nailed whatever her heart and soul needed to say. It was a glorious and historic affair. In terms of a Minnesota icon being feted in their hometown, it was the closest thing I've witnessed to Bob Dylan's five-night run at the Orpheum Theatre in 1992. And it was just as special, as was she.

Minneapolis Star Tribune, June 28, 2013

Jeanne Peterson and Paul Metsa
(Photo by Jeff Miletich)

CHRISTMAS AT MOLLY'S

Twenty-fourth of December, as a stranger, I walked like I
just lost the keys to the city
As a stranger, I sent postcards 'round the world but the
picture tonight wasn't pretty

I walked in the shadows of haunted hotels like a miner
trapped in a cavern
but I looked to the East and a star, it
shown down, and it led me right to Molly's Tavern

So I followed the footprints made in the snow by
Salvation Army musicians
I got in line and stood right behind a tap dancer and two
blind magicians
You would have thought I had been there before, as
Molly stood there to greet me
Eighty years old and a gleam in her eye said, "you're
expected," and proceeded to seat me

Chorus

C'mon ye low-down rounders, lift up your low-down
Ways, pass the malt and the mistletoe, it's almost
Christmas Day

I walked around and the harp player asked if I
would like to request a selection
I smiled and I asked for "God Bless the Child" and for
him I took up a collection

I spotted a man with a white beard and red, from a
distance looked just like Kris Kringle
He went to the roof and I thought I heard hoofs and I
swear I heard sleigh bells a jingle

We waltzed on a dance floor made out of glass,
between dances we sang Christmas carols
Then we lit candles, had a moment of silence,
and the bartender read F. Scott Fitzgerald

Molly said first we must give to receive, we put our
trinkets into the kitty
In went my compass and my grandfather's watch, and I
pulled out the key to the city

Repeat Chorus

And so I guess if there's a lesson, I've learned it is one
that will keep me from danger
Sometimes you get lost just so you will be found
and return the kindness of strangers

I explained how I felt as I kissed Molly's
hand like a miner freed from a cavern
"Merry Christmas baby," is what she said to me
"but it's like this each night in my tavern"

So I sail on the oceans and I look at the sky
        and it seems like the whole world's on fire
And I just want to make angel wings in the snow
        and sing this song in that midnight choir

Repeat Chorus

Words and Music by Paul Metsa
Paul Metsa Music – 2018 – BMI ©

Molly Spaun, Owner of Molly's Bar, and Paul,
Superior, WI, December 24, 1989
(Photo by Dick Blin)

SUMMER

Summer days fade into early twilight
Slippery leaves become crisp and crumble
between honest hands and fingers

Green, red, and gold give way to brown
and soon to dust
so fast, so old, and then forgotten

Wind carries what is left in this universe
all that was bought and sold

The ancient age receives them back in silent whispers Where
have you been my silent leaves
A seed again
now welcomed home

BLACKIE AND A WOMAN'S TEARS (A LETTER TO MY SISTER)

Dearest Jackie,

So, I had kind of a tough week last week. Nothing worth going into, nothing out of the usual – a little heartbreak, and the music biz with another kick to this well-worn ass. A little dust-up with the greatest sister God has had the grace to give me, and Dad going to the doctor, which works out well but reminds me of his and our fragility.

So, this week starts out a little better, 'cause like they say, what a difference a day makes. Renea came over last night; she had finally finished Blackie's Christmas letter (or maybe by now his St. Patty's Day letter). She has a little belly on her, due in July. She looks beautiful and I wonder why in the hell I was not able to give my heart to this Oklahoma Rose. She helps me set up my printer, we get caught up on family, and I go out and buy her a candy bar.

Blackie, who I dressed in a snazzy red kerchief for the occasion, as usual, goes crazy when he sees her. If not for her, there wouldn't be him. He is such a ladies' man. He jumps up and down, does the Blackie dance, and snuggles up to her and rubs against her, looking into her eyes with those beautiful brown moonbeam eyes of his. They adore each other. May my own memory someday serve me as well.

Before she leaves, and he knows when she is going, he goes back to her for a last round of doggie hugs. She reaches down to give him a goodbye embrace. She is living by herself, and she tells me that things are fine between her and her fiancé, but in retrospect I don't know if I noticed her new engagement ring. And maybe, and I hope, she was still wearing it. As she hugs him, I notice she is crying, and a tear drops down on Blackie's nose, which he recently bruised in Heather's kennel in Duluth. The skin is worn off, and if it doesn't grow back, it is cute enough. I know her hormones are doing the mommy dance; she does love and miss Blackie, and maybe something more. I do not know. Perhaps it is the dew of hearts in passing.

We did share a family, the three of us, for a couple of years, sweet as the fruit of Eden. And Blackie had both a mom and dad. And she is moving on, a little girl growing within her. And I am an emotional weakling, swinging from the branch of fate, ready to drop at the slightest hint of wind.

It was but a minute in an 1890-built house somewhere in northeast Minneapolis, but I am no stronger today than yesterday, and I am remembering there is nothing stronger than a woman's tears. And I try to stay strong in this wicked world.

So, I come home tonight, and Blackie has had his way with the garbage can – coffee grounds, cigarette butts, and empty tin cans strewn across the kitchen. I have a piece of prime rib, a left-over from a friend's plate at Nye's Polonaise Room (I was there on business – no really, I was) that I am ready to share with Blackie, but am trying to find the responsibility within myself to discipline my dog. He meets me in the kitchen, I see the mess, and I raise my voice. Blackie looks at me, with those same brown eyes, and shudders like he must have when he was kept outdoors all day and night in the icy Northern Minnesota rain – when nobody came to play, and he felt no human hand on his musty fur – and wondered why no one was able to love him.

He backs into and under the back of my desk, knowing he did something wrong, but in doggie logic, has no idea what. It was, after all, the smell of food at nose level. It is not the first time he has eaten out of a garbage can.

I pour a glass of wine, run upstairs to make sure my new renter has all the keys for all the doors, and come back down. Blackie has moved to the bedroom, on his green Mexican ratty quilt on the floor. I go in, kneel down, and tell him why garbage diving is not what good dogs do. He looks up to me, and I pretend he at least understands a bit of what I am saying. His brown eyes tell me he might be lying, but also tell he loves me nonetheless. I go to the fridge, grab the prime rib, and split it with him, piece by piece, cross-legged on the floor.

He is now sleeping under the desk. I will go to Menard's tomorrow and buy a metal trash can with a lid, so as not to tempt him. It is a dog's world, and I am all right with that. I admire him from my chair, his paw softly beneath his jaw, dreaming those doggie dreams of trash cans with no lids, his mother in every room and, presumably, peace on earth. And the bruise on his nose seems to be disappearing, perhaps slowly being cured by the rarer visits of his loving mother's salty tears.

Love you,
Paul

Blackie
(Photo by Amy Donlin)

MITCH OMER

Last New Best Friend

◆ A Tribute ◆

"Come on in my kitchen, it's gonna be rainin' outdoors."

Mitch Omer's reputation preceded him. Years of working through the rungs of kitchen jobs near and far produced the driven and primarily self-taught master chef, who opened Hell's Kitchen in downtown Minneapolis in 2002.

For several years on every other Sunday or so, I had visited a little breakfast nook below the violin shop, next to the drum shop and across from Schmitt's Music, for my leisurely musician's brunch. My Sunday solo brunches, beginning around 11 a.m., included a bit of a secular meditation on my work and station in life, as I ordered my usual: coffee and small milk, two eggs over easy, hash browns well done with cheese, sausage links, and whole wheat toast with peanut butter. With that, I was able to accomplish two things: raise my cholesterol count to its monthly limit in two visits, and enjoy the fact that, after years of struggling, I could enjoy a fine breakfast and leave a fat tip. As they say, the little things in life make it worth living.

Then one Sunday the restaurant had changed hands. The name was changed to Hell's Kitchen. It was now a cutting-edge restaurant with Ralph Steadman's artwork (Hunter S. Thompson's illustrator and partner in crime) painted on the walls, a twist on the standard breakfast fare, and homemade peanut butter that could bend one's knees to thank Heaven for toast and all that is good on Earth. My new buddy Mitch Omer (whom I actually wouldn't meet until 13 years later) created it, and it was my first glimpse at his genius.

Mitch Omer became a celebrity chef in Minneapolis years before chefs were celebrated. I read his name in the newspapers and magazines that kept tabs on the evolving Twin Cities' foodie culture and cuisine, but for years had never had the pleasure to meet him.

That changed in 2015 when my ensemble, the Paul Metsa Soul and Blues Revue, was booked to play New Year's Day 2015 at Hell's Kitchen at their new location on 9th St. and Marquette in downtown Minneapolis (formerly Rossi's Blue Star Room). About six weeks earlier, to put the logistics of the gig together, I met with the president of Hell's Kitchen, Pat Forciea, a fellow Iron Ranger whom I got to know when he was working with the late great Paul Wellstone. While waiting for Pat at the host stand, I started to read Mitch's cookbook *Damn Good Food*. The front pages contained an amusing letter to the editor that told about two couples from the East Coast who were winter camping in the Boundary Waters Canoe Area when they spotted a naked 400-pound Yeti cross-country skiing up on a ridge. I would find out later that was Mitch.

Back to Mitch. After a falling-out with his father over quitting the Iowa State football team in 1972, where he was attending on a full scholarship, Mitch headed north to Ely, Minnesota, where he and his father had camped in the 1960s. There he was taken under the wing of Earl Bulinksi, Sr., who gave him a place to stay in exchange for work. Mitch fell in love with Ely. He helped start the Chocolate Mousse Restaurant, hosted a show on WELY, and stayed for several years.

As my band started to play on that New Year's Day in 2015, a man entered the room – about 6 foot 5, silver white hair over his ears, wearing colored glasses, a black vest over a white shirt, cowboy boots, and a Stetson. It was the man himself, Mitch Omer. He sat on the steps next to the stage and listened to all of the last set. I could tell he was enjoying himself.

When we finished, I walked over and introduced myself. He couldn't have been kinder or more complimentary. As if twin brothers of a different mother, we connected instantly. We talked of Ely, the Iron Range, and realized we had friends, experiences, places and world views in common, as well as a mutual love of the blues. Mitch had even attended a gig I did at the Yugoslav National Home in Ely in 1997 (yearly membership was $2.00), the night the 100-year record for cold weather was broken – 60 below zero WITHOUT a wind chill!

I didn't want to take up more of Mitch's time, as he was there to sign copies of his cookbook. I did invite him to be a guest on my radio show the following week, kicking off 2015 in style, and very much looked forward to getting to know him and hear more of his life stories. I left Hell's Kitchen that afternoon basking in the glow of meeting a great new friend.

Mitch showed up at the studio a few days later to tape the show. He was wearing a black cowboy shirt embroidered in red. He had rolled up his sleeves, revealing several tattoos, the most noticeable a sketch of the Indian Motorcycle logo across his right hand. But about the Yeti thing. I had to ask him if it was true that he was seen cross-country skiing naked that February afternoon in 1977. (Mitch weighed almost 400 pounds in those days, with hair down to his waist.) He replied, "That is a complete lie. I was snowshoeing." I fell in love with the guy immediately.

Mitch was a very busy guy. When he wasn't working at the restaurant, he would experiment with new recipes at his industrial-sized kitchen at a gorgeous condo where he lived with his lovely wife, Cynthia. Appropriately, the condo was in the original Cream of Wheat building, which was beautifully restored. We chatted on the phone regularly, got together a couple of times, and emailed each other sharing one-liners and laughs. A message or phone call from Mitch Baby – as Sonny Barger, leader of the Hell's Angels, called him after meeting Mitch in an Oakland, California, bar (you can't make this stuff up) – was always a highlight of my day.

Last summer, Mitch started having health problems. He was constantly tired, his feet were swelling, and several visits to the doctor yielded no answers to his condition. Yet he soldiered on, making the best of it. We had the chance to meet up a couple of times, and I so enjoyed our conversations. An 'old soul,' he was funnier than hell and self-deprecating, two traits shared by most of my good friends.

At the end of August, I got a call from Beth Pierce at the Iron Range Tourism Board, asking me if I knew of anyone who would make a great keynote speaker for their upcoming Restaurant Awards dinner at Giant's Ridge. I told her, "I have just the guy for this gig!" I put her in touch with Mitch and she hired him as the featured guest speaker. Mitch called me and asked if I wanted to tag along. Of course, I did.

Mitch picked me up on Friday before the Sunday evening dinner. I hopped in his ride with a handful of music that I'd curated for the drive – Robert Johnson, Bob Marley, Muddy Waters, Bob Dylan, among others. We both brought our guitars and were looking forward to playing together for the first time, heading north for the Iron Range and Ely, and places where we'd left pieces of hearts and homes so many years ago.

Our first stop was a late lunch at the gas station/restaurant just east of the Carlton exit. They have an amazing hot pork sandwich that I wanted Mitch to try. After ordering, he told me a story of how he ended up in that very restaurant years earlier while hitchhiking from Ely, broke and having to borrow money from a truck driver to make it the rest of the way to the Twin Cities. The man could tell a story and had dozens of them, each one crazier than the last. We got to our beautiful suite at Giant's Ridge about an hour before the sun was setting. Mitch looked out the window and saw two men wearing blaze orange, who were traversing the edge of the woods. Upon closer inspection, we realized they were doing some late-season golfing and chuckled—we had officially arrived in Northern Minnesota.

Pat Forciea had given Mitch instructions for the trip: pick up some "Hot Air" from Canelake's Candies in Virginia, some potica (a Slovenian nut roll and traditional festive pastry) from the Sunrise Bakery in Hibbing, and eat dinner at Valentini's in Chisholm, a true trifecta of Range culinary delights. We took off Saturday morning for Virginia, bought the chunks of Hot Air and other chocolate delights, visited my mother's memorial garden near the shore of Bailey Lake, stopped by nephew Jason's house to see his remodeling job, and sipped refreshments at the Sports Page Bar on Chestnut Street. We drove to Hibbing, but the Sunrise Bakery was closed, so I took him on a tour past Dylan's house and past the old cemetery, where a century of harsh winters and heavy snows had tilted the tombstones and ghostly winds still whistled through the graveyard, fading the names and dates. We ended with dinner at Valentini's in Chisholm (I always go with the baked rigatoni), headed back to Giant's Ridge, and called it a night.

On Sunday we got up early and took the backroads to Ely. Mitch held sway in the driver's seat, regaling me with story after story while I manned the CD player. His body language and smile conveyed he was returning home. We had a great breakfast at a restaurant next to the Ely Surplus and walked around the corner to a leather shop where the widow of a very good friend of his was working, continuing her husband's craft of designing wallets and belts out of moose hide. Mitch bought me one on the spot. I have the feeling the belt will last longer than I do.

We got back to Giant's Ridge in plenty of time for the awards ceremony. Several years earlier, Mitch and the staff at Hell's Kitchen had cooked and catered a breakfast in Embarrass after hearing that the weather there would be "colder than the surface of Mars." It was a benefit for the Volunteer Fire Department and raised over $4,000 for them. Mitch was clad in firefighter's gear. With a butane torch, he singed the corner of a page in the Hell's Kitchen cookbook as part of the fundraising campaign and became Embarrass's first "volunteer fire-starter." We were joined at the table that night by two of the women from that event, and Mitch was welcomed like MacArthur coming back to the Philippines.

After the awards, Mitch strode gently to the center of the room, sat on a chair, and with a handheld wireless microphone, he held forth. The gist of his message was that of all the things he had learned after four decades in the restaurant business, the most important thing was to treat each employee with kindness and respect. It was as simple as that.

That night, Mitch was tired and wanted to rest. I met up with an old friend in the nearby town of Biwabik. When I later returned to the hotel, Mitch had fallen asleep on his bed in the clothes he'd been wearing earlier (damn near the same get-up he was wearing when I met him). I pulled him up to his pillow and covered him with a blanket. If he wasn't a 61-year-old man, I would have read him a good-night story. The next morning, Mitch was up early and started playing his guitar. He was a damn good slide player. While we were planning on playing together at some point during the weekend, I enjoyed instead a private concert through a closed door. After listening for about 20 minutes, he serenaded me back to Dreamland. He didn't know he had an audience, and the serenity of the moment was mine alone to enjoy.

We stopped by the Sunrise Bakery in Hibbing later that morning, picked up the legendary potica, and headed back to the Twin Cities, back to work and the buzz of urban life. Mitch seemed recharged by the whole experience, and we brainstormed all the way back on how we could work together on projects we would soon invent. But it was not to be.

Mitch had more doctors' visits in his future, with still no idea what he was suffering from. I was honored that he made my 60th birthday party in downtown Minneapolis on November 1, sitting quietly at the bar and enjoying the music. We kept making plans to get together, but our schedules didn't allow it. On December 14, I got an email message from Mitch saying, "We need to get together before Christmas." I so would have enjoyed that. Instead, I was stunned to get the message that Mitch had passed away peacefully in his sleep on December 18, 2015.

Hell's Kitchen held his memorial service on December 23 at the restaurant. The place was packed, and the line went out the door to the host stand. The room was brimming with love and bursting with loss. I played guitar in the bar after the service while people were enjoying, of course, an amazing buffet. Pat Forciea gave a heartfelt eulogy and came up to me while I was leaving. "You were Mitch's last new best friend." I choked up. "He was mine as well."

Often with the loss of a friend, family member or loved one, you have the benefit of years of memories that help soothe the pain. Losing Mitch like this, for me, is more like mourning memories that we never had time to make. I feel blessed to have known the man, a true brother, and kindred reckless, generous, and artful spirit.

Hometownfocus.us, January 8, 2016

Paul Metsa and Mitch Omer
(Photo by Scott Streble)

BLACK CADILLAC

Delilah called me long distance from a hole
Black cloud over Roosevelt throwing sevens on a roll
Hercules handshake Chesterfields as they linger
You could bet on his luck like rings right down through
his finger

Copacabana, we danced in the street,
we played Woody Guthrie to the chief of police
Old strippers' street cries drown out drunk singers
You can bet on the love like rings on your finger right
down through your finger

Chorus

And you go where the angels go, on the back of a buffalo
Electric wings you'll fly on the birds of paradise
Birds of paradise

I dream black Cadillac bow tie right on Sunday,
old hymns for the astronauts lost right down on the
runway
Search party light out in the dark for you
When I close my eyes tonight, I see Roosevelt blue
Gone on a night train out of town on a rail,
cowboys can't find you tumbleweeds right down on your
Trail
Sweetheart's gonna miss you, she had you longer than
most
You can bet on the love like the rings right down on your
fingers,
you gotta give up the ghost, give up the ghost.

Repeat Chorus

Words and Music by Paul Metsa

IF JUNIOR MINTS COULD TALK

They would rather, then, be sweet
with something inside like coconut-
neither plant nor fruit –
maybe both

Hard-headed like poets
like guitar players
but silent and hiding behind tiny chocolate submarines

Like Kitty Kats and City Cats
sweet juice, almost too sweet, if that's possible
in a way and in a world, we will never know

But we know this one, I think
Breath on breath, mouth to mouth
Then heart beating,
as we know the world as is
as one

If we had nothing left to lose
there would be no cards left on the table.

THE STONE PONY INCIDENT

I stole a barstool from the Stone Pony. Religious pilgrims go to places like Mecca, Jerusalem, or the Great Pyramids to reaffirm their religious beliefs, but to my friend "Tilt" Rubin and me, musical pilgrims of modern America on a journey to places like Rosa's Blues Lounge in Chicago, The Continental Club in Austin, and The Stone Pony in Asbury Park, that red barstool represented everything that we liked about the Church of Saturday Night. Realizing that the statute of limitations might be different in New Jersey and this crime of passion may still be under investigation, I have been advised by my lawyer to not discuss the facts of the case. But in an effort to clear my name, please allow me to tell you of April 7, 2001, events played out under a Jersey Shore moon, the story of the alleged crime, heretofore referred to as "The Stone Pony Incident." My buddy and Jersey boy Joe D'Urso had invited me to play a benefit at The Stone Pony. I accepted the invite with both excitement and the purest of intentions.

It all started in a borrowed, and damn near undriveable, 1991 Subaru Wagon – definitely not a pink Cadillac – somewhere just north of the Bronx. We crossed over the George Washington Bridge and onto the New Jersey Turnpike, and for all intents and purposes, we could have been in a fever-dream-state-opening-sequence of *The Sopranos*. Gas refineries, hot asphalt, Jersey wetlands, toll booths, and fellow travelers on their way to who knows where. It isn't hard to picture Bruce Springsteen riding these roads, somewhere between dusk and daybreak, steering wheel of his Camaro in one hand and the other switching from the radio to yellow legal pad on the empty passenger seat, jotting down streets-of-fire memories in shorthand, the same memories he's trying to escape. Now my secret agent/ rock and roller dream since I was a kid was to take my guitar and ride it around the world. Next stop, rockin' Johnny, Asbury Park.

American rock and roll started around a campfire in a dark and howling wind. It was blues, country and hillbilly music then. It wasn't until it started raining and they moved it inside did it transform into something that became rock and roll. Now a wise man once said that "jazz is nothing more than two guys smoking pot in a small apartment," and he was on to something. There is something about music played inside four walls. Juke joint, rent party apartment, grease garage, or some full moon Ozark Barn Dance, you can hit a hot note on a cheap guitar and watch it bounce, back and forth in a volume echo. Gutbucket whiskey passed around in coffee cans, smoke from hand-rolled cigarettes misting blue windows, that both invite and keep the night at bay.

Beautiful women writhe to imaginary lovers on sawdust dance floors, strong young men on a weekend pass from some hell-forbidden job do the hucklebuck and chicken strut, the rhythm elevates and the string band in the corner jacks it up like drill hammers toward heaven. People fall in and out of love; a fistfight or two; a lonely tear is shed in the 3-D jukebox of the sons and daughters of Saturday night. Someone's making whoopee in a makeshift parking lot. The promoter-house papa pays the band, makes a little for him and the missus, and a sweaty crowd stumbles out sanctified and satisfied on the bye-and-bye into just another American night. So go to church on Sunday, 'cause the eagle won't fly 'til Friday.

The Stone Pony grew out of scenes like this. It was clubs like the Pony and others that kept this country rockin' since your Daddy or Granddaddy came back from World War II. They witnessed magic on a semi-regular basis, anytime some roadhouse band turned the joint into a high voltage promised land where all dreams may come true. It can, and has, happened anywhere, but according to myth and rumor, a little more so at the Stone Pony. Turn on the bright lights, baby, I'm on my way.

There is not a working musician who does not admire Bruce Springsteen. And it is not because he is for the blue-collar cat, but he is, in fact, a blue-collar cat himself. A blue-collar, highway-bound cool rockin' hound dog who came up through these highways and byways, his trusty Telecaster always by his side. Starlit neon lounges with the occasional Cadillac in front, with bands on matchbox stages playing to drunks, gracious ladies of the evening, semi-professional boxer bouncers, shark-suited business types, and tourists on their way to somewhere else. The band plays four or five sets for a bar tab and dreams of Elvis. There is a little bit of the midway left in Asbury Park and those faded memories mixing with the salty Atlantic breeze.

My first image of Asbury Park was the crumbling painting of Tilly, sad-happy clown, faded from years of neglect, yet a resolute emblem of a simpler America at play. As we rounded the corner and headed to the Stone Pony, I swear I saw Tilly wink at me. I winked back.

Tilt and I entered through the side door of the Stone Pony and were led backstage to meet the other performers and check set times. It was the first time I had set eyes upon her. Red vinyl ripped at the knee, round, firm and fully packed, legs long and lanky, with a glimpse of metallic nylon. She was about to be left behind by this no-time-for-nostalgia society still longing for a place to fit in, and next to the back door, dumpster bound like the chivalrous man that I am, I was determined to save this damsel in distress, and give her one more twirl 'round the dance floor.

7:00 p.m. soundcheck: As they were setting my monitor mix, I motioned for my 'manager' to come to the side of the stage. "Tilt, there is a red bar stool next to the back door. We're taking her home." As I finished the sound check, Tilt left to case the fenced-in parking lot, charting our escape route. We then reconvened at the bar and ordered drinks from a classic Jersey babe – same order, thank you – double Southern Comfort on the rocks. It was obvious that Kristi, the gorgeous bartender, had probably broken more hearts than Springsteen when he fired the E Street Band. I left Tilt to fall in love with a Jersey girl because I had a gig to do, sha-la-la-la.

Armed with a double shot of SoCo, a capo, songs cut from the psychic cloth of America, and my trusty Takamine – which I was to find out during the show is the Official New Jersey State Guitar – I was finally on that stage. That stage that has witnessed some of the finest rock and roll this country has had to offer, Saturday night soul shouts from the Jersey shore. And it was Saturday night, and I was ready to rock.

Artistically, this is where it gets a little hazy. I was about to play on a stage graced by the likes of Springsteen, Little Steven, Southside Johnny, Joey Ramone, Bob Stinson and only God knows who else, and all I could think about was stealing that damn barstool. We all remember the hotel terry cloth bathrobes or fancy monogrammed ashtrays our folks would bring back from vacation, slipping the contraband into their suitcases and bringing them home. This was a little different. There was one big-ass bouncer, and a 15-foot-high chain link fence between the stool and the trunk of my borrowed car.

And to say nothing of my reputation as a musician who would like another gig on the Eastern Seaboard, I was genuinely honored to be playing there. But believe me, this was a twisted, Southern Comfort-fueled rock and-roll-five-finger discount of the highest order. It also had the potential for an incredibly negative karmic comeuppance.

WWED - What Would Elvis Do?

Now amidst the meticulous planning for this caper was a wonderful benefit show featuring some incredible performers: a NYC legend; a famous folkie from England; myself; Jersey homeboys Bobby Strange, Bruce Tunkel, and Joe D'Urso, whose Springsteen influence was just a shot away. There were elements of his songcraft, performance style, delivery, and even dress code floating through his Garden State brethren. Willie Nile, in particular, was absolutely spellbinding, fire and brimstone, manic wordsmith, and as funny as early Mort Sahl (buy all his records). Tilt and I were walking the tightrope that separates James Bond from Foster Brooks. As our SoCo consumption was reaching double digits, a huge rumble came over the impeccable house sound system.

Seemingly out of nowhere, the live version of the newly released *Springsteen: Live in New York City* came with *"Born to Run"* on 11 (and oddly just came up on my CD player as I am writing this sentence), blasting through the room and to the moon. It was an incredible moment, many of us hearing this version for the first time. We were landlocked in a brilliant revelry in which strangers sometimes find themselves transported, as a group, to somewhat higher ground – this night, this time, I think I could rightfully say into the heart and soul of New Jersey.

After six solid hours of Stone Pony time, Tilt and I decided to get some air and check out another club. There was still another hour 'til the encore. Our neighborhood choices were an empty cowboy bar, a bar featuring male strippers with an inordinate amount of guys in the audience, and a hip-hop strip club that had our name all over it – Tupac Shakur at 130 decibels and a liberal door policy concerning the clientele (hell, they let us in). There were two dancers working a small stage in the inner rectangle of the bar. They were shaking and quaking the bacon like nothing I had ever seen nor dreamt about. They were easily as large as most high school linebackers and their G-strings seemed like an afterthought. One of them, out to show the honkies a good time, came up to our place at the bar, placed one leg in front of us in a stretch that would make Jackie Joyner-Kersee jealous, and started to gyrate until my fillings were loose. Tilt and I were in complete agreement: these were the "heaviest…and the hottest" strippers we had ever seen. We tipped like drunken sailors and hightailed it back to the Pony.

We entered the club as the hard-travelin' Dave Sharp, formerly of The Alarm, was wrapping up the show. The room was packed with fans looking to "Rock the City" for Charlie McIntosh's good cause: The Royal Manchester Children's Hospital. There were strong rumors of a possible appearance by the Boss himself. Turned out the Boss was having a private release party at his place. Special guest or not, the show must, and did, go on. The night ended with a stacked stage, 25 strong, each of us putting our signature on a twenty-minute encore that served as both a Chuck Berry love letter to the audience and a collective high five of our shared influence. Go Johnny Go!

After having completed the job that I had been invited here for, I was now able to dedicate the remainder of my quickly dwindling faculties to the heist. After a quick huddle, and one more SoCo to bolster our confidence, it was now or never. As I engaged the back-door security guard in small talk (which represented the absolute last of my rap), Tilt grabbed the stool and beelined through the shadows to the fence. Blood alcohol levels be damned, our next move was no less than Tinkers-to-Evers-to-Chance meets Willie Sutton. In a move that would have given Richard Kimble flashbacks, Tilt 'gracefully' climbed the fence with one arm, the other clinging proudly to our soon-to-be rock and roll prize. I had quickly made my way back through the crowded club to the other side. From 15 feet up, in the Asbury air, Tilt guided the stool over the top of the fence and into my awaiting, open arms. Tilt's victory leap to the pavement is now the stuff of legend—in fact, the morning after the heist, the 15-foot jump had already increased to 20 feet.

We made it back to our hotel, the Berkeley Carteret, with one red stool, one guitar, a Joan Jett Stone Pony sidewalk poster, two coffee cups, four barbecued pork sandwiches and two large impending hangovers. The legendary Convention Hall, across the way from the hotel, had hosted a headbangers marathon earlier that evening. The hallways of the hotel resembled something out of *The Night of the Living Dead*. We fit right in.

We cashed out around 4 a.m., weary from four days of travel and 'work' culminating in what the state of New Jersey deems subpoena-worthy. Two hours later, karma started to rear its ugly head. Our telltale heart materialized as a disorienting blast louder than a LaGuardia Airport runway directly outside our door, interrupting what would have been my first solid night of sleep in four days. I called the front desk to describe this ear-shattering music cascading through the halls, as though Motorhead was practicing in the next room, an Atlantic Ocean foghorn from hell. "Dude," the desk clerk respectfully replied, "it's a fire alarm."

I replied as politely as a sleep-deprived, alcohol-soaked fugitive from-the-law folk singer could, "Can you shut the GOD-DAMN THING OFF?!?"

"Not until the Asbury Park Fire Department gets here," he said.

Fifteen minutes later, the sonic hell subsided. My head, already feeling like cracked maracas, fortunately did not explode. Tilt, of course, slept through the whole episode.

We checked out without incident (OK, we stole the room key) and had a hangover-cure breakfast worthy of John Barrymore: two eggs over easy, cheese on the well-done hash browns with onions, rye toast with peanut butter, small steak, coffee, orange juice, and water, lots of water. Frank's Deli did us right and we were on our road to, if not redemption, at least recovery. We were served by a waitress, who through our Ray Bans looked to be the next Miss New Jersey. One stop left before the Stone Pony Incident was behind us.

We stopped to gas up and buy cigarettes at a station that had seen better days but was still full service. The attendant, a brother named Hollywood with a guard dog as ugly as he was handsome, came out in the salt mist of the Asbury Park morning air to fill our tank. He hipped us to the fact our tires were almost out of air, and we were riding damn near on the rims. He noticed the guitar and bar stool in the back seat, and we proceeded to tell him the story. With our tank and tires full, we were ready to make our rock and roll getaway. We laid a Jefferson on the brown-eyed handsome man and as we were leaving, he gave us the Tilly wink and said, "Your secret is safe with me."

Paul Metsa (with help from Tony "Tilt" Rubin).
Special thanks to Joe D'Urso for inviting me to play the gig.

DAVE MORTON

◆ *A Tribute* ◆

"When another student was ready, the teacher reappeared."

Dave Morton was an American original. He was a natural mystic, an artist, poet, musician, songwriter, bandleader, performance artist, visionary, and a beatnik to his core. He was also a family man, and toward the last 30 years of his working life, a construction worker specializing in laying cement. Whatever station he found himself in life, he inspired those around him to lead a more meaningful life, and like the jazz man that he was, improvised it all along the way. A gentler man I have never met.

He came of age in Minneapolis, Minnesota, nurtured by liberal Unitarian parents who took their 7-year-old son to see one of Lead Belly's last shows at Northrop Auditorium on the University of Minnesota campus in 1948. Ten years later, he became a mellifluous cultural force bridging the Beat scene with the years-away hippie scene from his base in Dinkytown, off the U of M campus. He was steeled politically as one of the original Freedom Riders, and shared a hot Mississippi jail cell with future longtime political activist Marv Davidov and a handful of other white folks who bussed down to Mississippi to cross the color line, desegregating interstate bus travel in 1961.

I met Dave Morton on my first day working construction in June of 1976. I had no idea what to expect, and although the money was good, I really wasn't looking forward to it. I arrived at the Forbes Taconite Plant, parked my car, and checked in. They gave me a bright blue hard hat and pointed me to the bus that was to take us to the job site. I got on the bus and felt that between my long blonde hair and the shiny hard hat, I was the proverbial lamb entering the lion's den. I wasn't wrong.

The bus was full of hardcore red iron workers, most from out of state, who had travelled to Northeastern Minnesota to build the taconite mines in the last great construction boom for the area. As I entered the bus, the aroma of stale beer and whiskey emanating off the assembled, after yesterday's hard day of work and a harder night at the local bar, nearly knocked me out. Most of them were wearing work clothes that were worn day after day, and most holding lunch pails large enough to feed a family of four, faded tattoos barely visible on arms like railroad ties.

Lord help me. As I was walking toward the back of the bus, I spotted him. In the back row was a tall, gangly gentleman, with a beatific smile and a handlebar mustache, carrying a children's Munster's lunch bucket. A possible kindred soul. I took a deep breath, now ready to meet the day ahead.

That afternoon I ended up on a cement pour. I was the grunt, carrying brick and block, wheelbarrow after wheelbarrow of cement, to the guys who put the finishing touches on it. There he was, my soon-to-be lifelong friend and confidant, in knee pads and covered in dust. There was a 15-minute union break and I introduced myself. It just so happened he lived on a farm less than a mile from the original Metsa homestead in Angora, Minnesota, and was the handyman for my Aunt Lilian, who still lived there. Before we started the last shift of the day, he told me a quick story about how his band, the Jook Savages, played at the Winterland in San Francisco on Halloween in 1967, and helped roll out Janis Joplin hidden in a Moroccan carpet before she started her set. Obviously, this was a man with a story to tell.

At the time, I was playing with my band *Cats Under the Stars* (formerly *Hot Walleye)* and occasionally sharing shows with the *Pike River Bottom Boys*, an acoustic quintet of Northern Minnesota boys who specialized in their versions of bluegrass, country tunes, and originals. They were usually as stoned as *The New Riders of the Purple Sage* and played some of their songs as well. We played local bars and taverns, and my favorite, old country dance halls. My grandfather, Emil Metsa, serenaded country folk decades before with his accordion at these same dance halls, often walking several miles through the woods to get there. Dave and the Jook Savages, the ever-evolving, loose-limbed and ever-changing jug band of acoustic warriors that always included the all-important jug player, were often featured as well.

In retrospect, they remain some of the most fun gigs I've ever played: honest music, played without pretension or rehearsal, for free-spirited dancing fools, recalling an earlier era and smothered in clouds of homegrown marijuana. The real and newly emerging New America, patriotic as any generation before them.

While 'Mort' and I spent the rest of the summer working together, hanging occasionally at his farm (while getting to know his lovely wife Shirley and his two lovely young daughters, Larkspur and Maja) and playing those gigs, I really had no idea of the depth of his history and influence. That changed in 1978 when I moved to Minneapolis. Every musician I met on the West Bank, many who got their start in the folk music breeding ground of Dinkytown, had a Dave Morton story.

In Robert Shelton's Bob Dylan biography *No Direction Home*, he referred to Morton's influence on Bobby Zimmerman in the first pages of the book as "when the student is ready, the teacher will appear."

Morton was the first act to play at the legendary 10 O'Clock Scholar coffeehouse, the site of the genesis of the soon-to-be Holy Trinity of Koerner, Ray and Glover, and home to some of Dylan's first gigs. Morton was tight with 'Diamond' Dave Whittaker, the man who turned Dylan on to Woody Guthrie. According to Mort, he told Dylan one night after a jam session, "I like your stuff, but you should consider writing your own songs." We all know how that turned out. In fact, Whittaker and Mort gave the young Iron Ranger a ride to the edge of town as Dylan, guitar in tow, hitchhiked out to New York City to meet his idol, Woody Guthrie.

Besides writing songs based on the melodies and structures of old folk and blues tunes, Dave wrote poetry and would sometimes read them at parties, completely naked, as that is just how parties rolled back then. He also painted, made jewelry, and created artful collages. In the buttoned-down mind of those times, Dave started growing his hair and beard, and was not too shy to wear a bathrobe while walking the streets of Dinkytown amidst others in their suits and ties. There is a great picture of Mort, wearing an American Flag as a cape at an art show, that embodies the free-flowing spirit of the time.

He then ended up in San Francisco, in the nascent days of Haight-Ashbury, in 1966. He started up a West Coast version of the *Jook Savages*, falling in with the *Grateful Dead*, the *Jefferson Airplane*, Janis Joplin, and the *Sons of Champlin*, back when acid was legal, love was free, and the world seemed to be evolving into a much better place.

His footprints there are documented in a variety of places. The *Jook Savages* are mentioned in Tom Wolfe's novel *The Electric Kool Aid Acid Test*. Rick Griffin, one of the most noted early psychedelic poster artists, included them on his first poster advertising a benefit for the Oracle, a Haight-Ashbury head shop and newspaper. Mort tells the story of how the Savages ended up at the Watts Acid Tests with the Grateful Dead in Watts, L.A., at the height of the riots, where they were all too stoned to play. *Frank Zappa and the Mothers of Invention* shared a gig with the Savages and one of them remarked, "You make the *Mothers of Invention* look like the *Beach Boys*!"

He and his wife Shirley bought 40 acres in northern Minnesota, a mile down the road from the original Metsa homestead, in 1971 – true pioneers of the back-to-the-land movement. The first thing that Shirley and Dave did was join the Unitarian church. A spiritual searcher, with one foot in the past and one, with a buck dancer's choice high step, into the future. A natural leader, with no quest for power, he put together the next version of what would become several incarnations of the *Jook Savages*, hosting house parties and saunas on regular Saturday night hootenannies. The jams took place in the kitchen of their 80-year-old farmhouse, chickens and stray dogs circling the property with full run of it all, and Shirley often manning the jug.

Dave's presence on the Iron Range was always greeted with smiles from anyone he came in contact with. Be they fellow construction workers, any regular man or woman on the street, bankers or bartenders, and all in between, everyone who met him had a better day. He was the Good Time Charlie who you'd run into just when you needed to. His lifestyle, quiet power and perennial smile, magic and mojo, his ever-changing look of long hair, buzz cuts, mustache, long beard or short – his presence reminded us that all that matters is how you hold yourself and how you treat others.

Simply, Mort was ahead of his time on so many levels. I recognized that early on. He always kept abreast of my career, and perhaps saw a bit of himself, had he kept at it. Or maybe not.

FAST FORWARD

In a perfect confluence of American spirit and timing, Dave and my father, Elder Metsa, ended up in the same senior highrise in Cook, Minnesota, in the early part of 2000. Though neither men were as radical as either of them, imagine Richard Nixon and Abbie Hoffman ended up retiring together in the same retirement home. Kind of like that, except sweeter. They became good buddies, each riding out great lives in slow and beautiful moments. They watched out for each other.

If Dad had a little extra food, he'd run it up to the third floor to share with Mort. When Dad took several trips a week to the casino, Dave looked out of his window facing the parking lot to make sure Dad made it home okay.

It was the beautiful last fugue of two Americans, each with different paths in their American journey, enjoying twilight time within one floor of one another.

I was a little too young to be a hippie, but was inspired by that movement, as well as the hard work American way – do the right thing, work your ass off, and achieve the American Dream, like my father. I look back at both versions of the American Experience. They've both informed me.

I recognize that my station in life, as a musician and artist, have benefitted from the strength and bravery of my great grandfather, who emigrated from Finland to work in an underground mine in Soudan, Minnesota. He made enough money to build the Metsa homestead and raise five children, one who died at the age of two. One of his sons, Emil, my dad's father, owned a gas station/dry goods store, and then The Roosevelt Bar in Virginia, Minnesota, my hometown. He and his wife Elna raised their only son Elder, my dad, who grew up above the bar as an only child. Though college trained as a teacher, he ended up as not only a businessman, but also school board member, city councilperson, and served two terms as Mayor while raising me, my brother and my two sisters with my beloved mother Bess.

I gave up the offer to take over my dad's insurance real estate and insurance business to make my way in the world as a musician. Truth be told, there have been midnight moments when I wonder if I made the right choice. Like Van Morrison once said, "It doesn't matter what you've done, all that matters is that you are still around." Thank God I am. And in terms of other career choices at this age, I am too old to join the FBI.

Dave worked his ass off, and raised two lovely daughters who both teach college – Dr. Larkspur Morton, who works in environmental education, and Maija, in public radio, teaching journalism. His advice to them during their school years was, "Don't forget to sass your teachers."

I enjoyed that Dave and Dad lived just one floor apart, enjoying the fruits of their life and labors, in a senior home with others like them. Not a bad way to take that last ride home.

When I ponder what America has meant to me, I most enjoy all the opportunities and avenues this country has afforded us. I look back at both dad's and Dave's generations, at once at loggerheads, and wonder which generation won.

They made their mistakes, as I have mine. But at the end of this American day, I look at both of their generations as breaking stone cold even. Both journeys and paths worked. And that, my friends, is the beauty of America.

Elder Metsa, Dave Morton, Paul Metsa
(Photo courtesy of the Cook News-Herald)

DRUNKEN POETS

Are there not enough of them?
Have they not won any battles lately?
Or do they hang out in corners
smoking stolen cigarettes from older teenagers
And when all time stops

they are both younger than that, and older than any of
them or younger than that now, as we can only hope

Are they not doing anything more than listening to birds on their
way to somewhere else?
Everywhere, and then the great beyond and somewhere in between

Is that not what birds do, but they do keep flying? And even
when the wind is sleeping and gunshot meadows go black and all
of those birds lay back higher than the wind
lower like the dinosaurs that they knew would all die soon
enough And die they did or not?
Throwing one more long-necked kiss

Another green long-necked, slime-backed
awkward lover that understood them and
kissed them back

From across a pond, between birds
light, like a magician
that appears, then disappears
between a beating heart or two
kicked around in forgotten alleys
as all alleys should be
unlike hearts, that shouldn't be
but lingers in smoke
and clouds
and in both morning and midnight mist
Lingers
because it has to

YELLOW, RED AND BLUE

We did our best work after midnight just beyond last call
while the moon winked at us kindly and gave us a solid pass
the sunrise soon to kick our ass
tip jar money in both our pockets
will be spent soon enough
though money never mattered
that night or any other day
the invisible beauty between both still and beating hearts
liquid vibration and lines of love
art and life in common
we talked about our mothers
we shared the latest dirty joke
played bebop jazz on the midnight radio
just loud enough to not wake Babe
the octogenarian landlady who loved Danny Kaye
off in dreamland after listening to Boris Karloff
reel-to-reel tapes from another time
by firelight Tiffany lamps
who would soon be enjoying her daybreak breakfast
always a banana and oatmeal
there is a lesson in that
more brown whiskey medicine
as you deconstructed abstract expressions by
Rothko, Pollock, and your favorite, Franz Kline

spontaneous brush strokes and splashes
all touching the Divine
your Eye Jazz paintings, my Iron Range prairie songs
as we encouraged each other
and, dare I say, learned from each other as well
we stared into that crystal ball
knowing 30 years from now
you'd still be dripping paint
my songs still bouncing off the wall
and so it is, my friend
nothing ever changed
brother to brother midnight chants
before that stumble home
preserved now in electrum amber
and all things being equal
we beat the fucking odds

Written for and dedicated to James Wrayge

MILLION DOLLAR BASH 2001

In 2001, I organized and helped promote a 60th-birthday tribute to Bob Dylan at First Avenue in Minneapolis. I wrote an article for On the Tracks, *a quarterly Dylan fan magazine out of Colorado. This is an excerpt from that article.*

This was almost going to be about Istanbul. Sometime in March of 2001, I received an email inviting me to play at a Bob Dylan Birthday Tribute at a horse farm in Turkey. Say what you will about the modern Jewish troubadour, but after he left his two-story stucco house in Hibbing in 1959, he began to write songs that were heard clear as a bell and louder than gunshots around the whole world. I grew up in Virginia, Minnesota, on the Iron Range (twenty-one miles east of Hibbing). One Saturday afternoon, while in second grade, I snuck downtown and saw Elvis in *It Happened at The World's Fair* at the Maco Theater, and my life was forever changed. Elvis played guitar, drove nice cars, hung out with beautiful women. With all due respect to Harmon Killebrew, the Minnesota Twins homerun king, I now had another role model worth emulating. I begged my folks for a Sears Silvertone guitar with a cowboy and horse stenciled on the front, and with that, was on my way.

Dylan on the radio in 1965 was like a Buck Rogers laser shot. Mama was in the basement mixing up the medicine and the rest of us walked the shadow streets of this New America, seduced and enchanted by these new wild and mercury sounds. Those sounds changed my life, your life, and how America viewed itself. When I got old enough to hitchhike, I'd catch a ride to Hibbing and stand in front of this house and wonder what ghosts haunted Bobby Zimmerman and turned him into Bob Dylan. Good for those ghosts, I say.

Although an all-expenses-paid trip to Istanbul to play Dylan tunes, and some of my own, to the Turkish faithful of His Bobness sounded like a hallucination worth having, I reconsidered.

Two martinis and a half a pack of Lucky Strikes later, it seemed obvious that Minneapolis owed its favorite folkie son a birthday tribute of the highest and most swinging order. The Million Dollar Bash, a Minneapolis Rock and Roll Hootenanny Tribute Show to Minnesota's hippest soon-to-be-60 rockin' cat daddy and native son, was informally underway.

The first call I made when I got home was to Kevin Odegard. Odegard was one of the guitarists on Dylan's *Blood on the Tracks* and had boldly suggested to Dylan that he change the key of "*Simple Twist of Fate*" from G to A, which he did. I have suggested to Odegard since that that should go on his tombstone. May we all have such moments in these mysterious lives of ours. I asked him if it was possible to get the boys back together from those sessions (including Bob Berg-drums, Gregg Inhofer-keys, Chris Weber-guitar, Peter Ostroushko-mandolin, and Billy Peterson-bass) for one set. They had not played together since those magical sessions in Minneapolis in 1974. Odegard was on it like cigarette burns on Keith Richards' Telecaster.

I had to leave for NYC in a few days and was looking forward to gigs at the Mercury Lounge on the Lower East Side and at the Stone Pony in Asbury Park, the former stomping grounds of Bruce Springsteen and others. While in NYC, a Vanity Fair article came out with an excerpt from a book by David Hajdu about the early '60s folk scene in Greenwich Village. While reading it, I realized that it was also the 40th Anniversary of Dylan's debut in Folk City. The flag of history was waving wildly. I also spent an afternoon with my friend Tony 'Tilt' Rubin at the Woody Guthrie Archives on 57th Street, in the august company of Harold Leventhal (Woody Guthrie's manager, who presented a young Bob Dylan at Carnegie Hall), Fred Hellerman (one of the original members of the Weavers), and my friend Nora Guthrie (Woody's daughter), who was in the process of putting Woody's vast archives together. And for those of you who don't know: No Woody Guthrie, No Bob Dylan – and it really is as simple as that.

When I got back to Minneapolis, I called Odegard, who told me everyone from the *Blood on the Tracks* sessions (now referred to as BOTT) was available with the exception of Bill Berg, drummer and also a Hibbing native. The concert was going to be Wednesday, May 23, the night before Dylan's actual birthday. I suddenly realized May 23 was also the seventh anniversary of my mother's death. Let her ghost and spirit guide me. After several days of rehearsal, along with Nate Kranz at First Avenue contacting and booking 40 other bands for the show, the concert was finally approaching.

The show started at 8 p.m. with Hugh Brown (one of Dylan's first roommates in Dinkytown) reading Dylan's "*Last Thoughts on Woody Guthrie*" (now repeat after me, No Woody, No Bob). Dave Morton, an early influence on Dylan, arrived on stage in a Hibbing baseball cap and proved he is the missing link between Jed Clampet and Salvador Dali. I also read a message from LeRoy Hoikkala, Dylan's first drummer from the Golden Chords, wishing us all the best. The place filled and some of the finest musicians in Minneapolis played, with inspiration and panache, choice covers for the Old and New Testament of America's greatest living songwriter.

The scene backstage was equally engaging: Cowboy hats and dreadlocks, spiked hair, long flowing curls, leather pants and wedding gowns, all nodding in unison to what each other had played or would be playing. And all silently agreeing with Paul Cebar, Milwaukee's finest musician, who put it so succinctly and spoke for these diamond-studded musical vagabonds, drifters and dreamers and back-alley poets, when he said, "Dylan, he ruined us all." It was a carnival, a revival meeting, a hipsters' prom, a séance, a street dance, a poetry reading and rock and roll hootenanny, shaken and stirred into one glorious night.

At 11 p.m. I introduced the Blood on the Tracks band. Listening to the opening salvo of "*Idiot Wind*" was like watching five prizefighters going for a knockout in the first round. "*You're a Big*

Girl Now" shone with the glow of thousands of midnight fireflies. By the end of "*Tangled up in Blue,*" the house, now 1,000 strong, was swaying in unison and shaking like a night train bound for glory. Dave Morton grabbed a tambourine, hopped up on stage and joined them, completing the circle from 1959 to 1974, all right here in 2001.

The midnight hour was now upon us and there was no way out for either the joker or the thief. The bands played louder, the audience dancing like the beach movie of your dreams, Dylan's words and melodies crashing against the walls like an unstoppable Holy Grail, through the roof and to the skies, in jungle rhythms of the damned and newly sainted in star-dappled circles from his hometown, this night, to the world. With crimson flames tied through my ears on a high and mighty trap, I played "*My Back Pages*" with Billy, Peter, and Gregg, dedicated it to Ma, and lead the thousand-voice Mill City Choir in the smoke-filled, whisky-drenched campfire chorus: "I was so much older then, I am younger than that now." Highway 61 now ran right through the center of town.

Six hours, forty acts and seventy-some songs later, the show closed with the grand finale, a sacred circle with Bob's musical messengers, those pilgrims tough enough to still be standing, and the rock and roll prayer, "I Shall Be Released." I was, and we were.

On the Tracks, August 31, 2001

Bob Dylan's 60th Birthday

REMEMBERING WEE WILLIE WALKER

◆ *A Tribute* ◆

"Singing made me really happy."

Willie Walker was one of the last great American soul singers, a ray of light from the right hand of God, my musical duo partner for almost ten years, and one of my dearest friends. We played over 500 gigs together, each one as fun as the last, sometimes more. We were joined at the hip through the magic of coincidence and the kindness of friends.

I had picked up a weekly gig at Rudolph's Barbeque at the corner of Franklin and Lyndale, less than a half block from my first apartment in Minneapolis. I had been doing several Thursday nights with another great soul singer, New Orleans born-and-bred Willie West (the Meters and Allen Toussaint), who, as fate would have it, married a gal named Pat Gambucci who grew up two doors down from me in my hometown of Virginia, Minnesota. They met at a nurses' conference she was attending. He was playing one of the private parties they were having. Pat, after several rum and cokes, grabbed his backside at some point, and they've been married 25 years. They moved from New Orleans to St. Cloud, Minnesota, to escape the carnage of Hurricane Katrina. Willie and I started playing together at Rudolph's, but after several gigs, West concluded that the 90-mile drive from St. Cloud was too long to make weekly. Enter our good friend Julia Schroeder, who suggested I call soul singer Willie Walker to fill in. Like many in the Twin Cities, I was well aware of the legend that was he (as a teenager, Prince used to listen to Walker and sit in at his gigs), but it hadn't dawned on me to call him. It was the kindest suggestion I have ever had the privilege to take up.

I called Walker and suggested he put up 10 to 12 songs he wanted to play, and I would suggest 10 to 12 of mine. He had his reputation and I had mine, and as gigs like this don't pay enough to require too much sweat, blood, and tears, I told him, "Let's pretend we're a really cool lounge act someone might find in a groovy bar in the 60's or 70's – no reason to overthink this." I went over to his house in East St. Paul at noon to find him in his kitchen, nursing a tumbler of brandy and watching old black-and-white cowboy movies with the sound off. We ran through a couple dozen songs which became our bedrock set list for the next ten years, adding new songs every now and then, usually busting them out on the gig without rehearsal.

The first set went off without a hitch, like sliding into a pair of old slippers. The most important element for any group of musicians is to connect rhythmically. After the first or second tune, our hearts beat as one. On the break, while smoking cigarettes on Franklin Avenue, we started to talk about numerology and the significance of numbers. He told me his favorite number was 33, "the age that my brother, Sam Cooke, and Jesus died." I could just feel this cat and I were meant to be together. Over the next ten years that we got to know each other, and the angelic depth of his spirit and musicianship shone through, that statement never left me. It was a beacon of things to come.

Though we played several big festivals and recorded a live record called *Live on Highway 55* (all first takes), our stock-in-trade was weekly gigs, most of them on Thursday evenings at Shaw's Bar, six blocks from my house in Northeast Minneapolis. It was my favorite night of the week. Though I lived closer, Willie usually got there before I did. When I got there, I could hear Willie's laugh cut through the club like a laser cutting steel, greeting all comers with something nice to say. Whether my week had been glorious or sucked eggs, Thursday was my happy place. Willie picked me up when I was down, and when feeling well, took me even higher.

We'd settle into our show, getting the bugs out of the sound system, Willie sipping his favorite E&J brandy, me my Christian

Brothers – his on the rocks, mine straight up. We played rhythm and blues chestnuts, blues classics, country songs, standards, and more. When Willie was in the mood and loosened up, he made "A Change is Gonna Come" his own personal anthem that I am sure made Sam Cooke smile from his grave. And while all sets went well, the pure gold of the experience with Willie was also chatting between songs and sharing the break on the patio. The guy had a terrific sense of humor, and at times had a rap as quick and poetic as Muhammad Ali.

Born December 23, 1941, Willie came from simple beginnings, growing up poor in Memphis, Tennessee, barbecuing hot dogs instead of ribs, as ribs and the rest were beyond his folks' ways and means. Though topping out at five-foot-two, he played football and boxed as a kid, and maintained his physique throughout his life. Whether dressed up for the big gigs, or down for the weekly shows, he was always impeccably attired. Nobody could rock a purple Vikings jersey (his favorite team) with a gold crucifix like Willie Walker on game day. He was pure class and never skipped a beat sartorially. Always a gentleman in the truest sense.

We'd play a tune or two and share stories or jokes between them. On drives to out-of-town shows, there were more laughs. Willie liked to tell stories about when he worked as a health care assistant. One was about a 108-year-old African American lady who'd occasionally put her legs up on the cafeteria table and say, "Willie, I NEED A MAN!" I loved that one, as did Willie. In the summer, he used to rent a pontoon boat on White Bear Lake, where he worked, and on his own dime, take as many residents as he could for a ride around the lake. Pure Willie, pure love. I asked him once when he realized how good he was. He replied simply, "It wasn't that really, but when I was about 12, I just realized singing made me really happy." He probably didn't realize at the time that for the next 65 years he would make the multitudes who heard him not only happy but would offer many a lifeline and coat of armor against the slings and arrows that life aims at all of us.

In 2016, harmonica player Rick Estrin was playing a gig at Famous Dave's Barbeque and Blues in Uptown Minneapolis. Julie Schroeder was driving Rick to a soundcheck in the afternoon and suggested they stop by Shaw's Bar to go and check out Paul Metsa and Willie Walker. He replied, "Not *the* Willie Walker? I have his late '60s singles. I thought he was dead!" They sat at the end of the bar right next to the stage. I saw Rick's face as he listened to Willie and thought he had seen a ghost. At one point, I could have sworn I saw a tear or two. One thing led to another, and Rick set Willie up with a record label with whom he recorded three albums. The reviews of all records were outstanding, and Willie started to tour the world, first as a supporting act, and soon after as a headliner: Brazil, Argentina, Paris, Spain, Italy, Scandinavia. Countries from around the world and all time zones welcomed him with open arms.

If I can take just a bit of credit, I know I helped keep his golden pipes intact weekly, and kept him singing, those pipes coming at the crowds like a Nolan Ryan fastball. One of my biggest joys was letting people hear that angelic voice backed by just a lone acoustic guitar. Heaven on earth.

As his fame grew worldwide, the Twin Cities treasure that was Willie Walker never changed a lick. He was as kind to the bartender, swamper or patron at Shaw's Bar as he was to the thousands that stood and cheered at all those festivals. Come one, come all; all are equal in the eyes of both Willie and God. I was always delighted to hear how all the tours went when he returned to the Twin Cities, and that in those last several years he finally got the credit he so richly deserved.

Several years ago, Willie and I did a concert at the historic Comet Theatre in Cook, Minnesota, that was run by my brother John and his wife Carol. It gave me the opportunity to stay at the Metsa cabin on Lake Vermilion and let Willie to do some fishing at the boathouse dock. Willie loved to fish, though he hadn't done so in years. I set him up with some bait, a chair, fishing rod, and a little E&J, and he spent several hours fishing there. Mid-afternoon I went to check on him. Willie grinned and pulled up the live chain with a dozen or so tiny fish. "What are you going to do with them – take 'em home and put 'em in your aquarium?" I asked. Hell, no. He cooked them up and we had a great dinner of crappies and perch.

The next night my brother invited us to his lodge at Pelican Lake for a barbeque. Willie and his second wife Judy had brought along Scooter, their little ankle-biter, to our cabin. I suggested to Judy it would be better to leave Scooter at the cabin on Vermilion, as my brother had two big dogs at his place and I didn't want any harm to come to Scooter. Judy got miffed and said, "I'm not going then!" Willie pleaded, "Judy, you've *gotta* come; I don't want to be the only Black person there!" Judy, for the record, is white. That is how deep their love was.

Another time, Willie had recently returned home from headlining the Porretta Soul Festival in Italy (which also featured Willie West). There'd been 20-foot-tall posters of Wee Willie Walker around the town. In a photo of him standing in front of one of the posters, Willie barely came up to his own knee. A week after that show, between songs on a gig at Shaw's, I asked Willie how many people were at that show in Italy. "About six thousand," he replied. I asked him, "How many people do you think are here tonight?" He smiled, took a sip of his E&J, and with a diamond gleam in his eye, through which you could almost see to Heaven, he said with a smile and chuckle, "Almost twenty." And that was Paul and Willie in a nutshell.

We had a terrific run playing our weekly gigs, festivals, funerals, benefits, backyard parties, and more. Willie electrified the crowd at the 2016 Humphrey-Mondale annual DFL fundraiser, held at the St. Paul Civic Centre, with a version of the Star-Spangled Banner that brought on a longer ovation than either Bernie Sanders or Hillary Clinton, whose speeches followed. At many of our shows over the years, Willie thrilled dozens of folks with his improvised vocal gymnastics on the Happy Birthday song that would give Mario Lanza a run for his money. I presented Willie Walker and West in concert the night they met for the first time in 2009. We played a long set of rhythm & blues standards, and they harmonized on the spot like two long-lost brothers. I still hope to put that recording out with the title *Paul Metsa Gives You the Willies*.

In November of 2019, Willie and Judy flew to California to record a third record with the Anthony Paule Orchestra. Willie did his last vocals on Saturday night and they headed home early Tuesday morning, arriving at 3 a.m. Judy slept for a few hours and went off to work as a nurse. She tried calling Willie several times that morning, and finally called the apartment supervisor, who went to check on him. Willie had passed away peacefully in his bed at age 77, in St. Paul, the city he called home for more than 50 years.

On December 22, a Celebration of Life was held in Willie's honor at the Minnesota Music Café, a club he played every other Sunday afternoon for more than 10 years. I made a call to the mayor's office in St. Paul, explained who Willie was, and suggested that they proclaim it 'Willie Walker Day,' which they did. It was an all-day event, and the place was packed to the gills, with some of the finest musicians in the Twin Cities paying respect to a man I referred to as the Godfather. I did a short set with Sonny Earl, Mari Harris, and Randi Starr Hudson – my longtime acoustic quartet. Willie West sat in at the end of the set and sang "What a Wonderful World" (a song Willie Walker owned when he sang it), and the 10-year circle of Willie West/Paul Metsa/Willie Walker was complete. The time we spent together, the laughter we shared, and the music we made were some of the greatest blessings God has offered me.

Yes, I think to myself, what a wonderful world…Oh Yeah!

Paul and Willie Walker
(Photo by Howard Christopherson)

AIN'T GONNA WHISTLE DIXIE ANYMORE

I saw your Tiki Torch parade on the blood red evening
news,
I remembered Timothy McVeigh and that Jesus was a
Jew,
Benedict Arnold waits for you in the hottest place in Hell,
The screaming souls will drown you out – your Sieg Heil
Rebel Yell

<u>Chorus</u>

Ain't Gonna Whistle Dixie Anymore, ain't gonna whistle
Dixie anymore
Bury that song in the land of cotton, deep in the Delta
mud to be long forgotten
Ain't Gonna Whistle Dixie Anymore

Fallen soldiers that were left behind, we salute on
wounded knee
Sacrifice of the highest kind, from Gettysburg
to Normandy
Burn your crosses, mask your face, sing the Appomattox
Blues
Woody Guthrie told us long ago, fascists are bound
to lose, fascists born and bound to lose

Repeat Chorus

Charlottesville Virginia, August 12th of '17
Emancipation Park and Dixie flags flew across the village Green
4 wheels of hate on 4th street raced where Heather Heyer died
Now her Blue Ridge Mountain Angel voice forever magnified,
forever magnified

Repeat Chorus

Words and Music by Paul Metsa
Paul Metsa Music – 2017 – BMI ©

FINGERTIPS

Stevie Wonder told us about our fingertips Soul
to soul, the best of that in darkness one love, and Bob
Marley too

Was this not our Catholic lesson?
Was this not our bow to a forgiving God?
whether we believed or not Wasn't there this
music in darkness then light

Wasn't there a dance floor that welcomed all of us
some drummer that called us all home some mother
waiting who knew we'd come home safe and sound?
Is this not faith, in our time and someone else's as well?

I scream in darkness but that is nothing new
I've heard the bells, those I've mentioned before

They ring as we speak, or talk silently in moments unforbidden
And I forbid none of them

Naked, swimming in waters warm and safe and sound

I scream to the mountains in silence
I play my guitar in shadows
Half of my heart beats now
And then, when she says hello
will beat later

And I write this as all poetry has been written in a darkened
corner, by candlelight soon to be blown out

That candle, in the morning, with her whisper in a shadow at
the break of dawn

LAST THANKSGIVING WITH DAD

"Remember to be kind and make someone happy."

I had the greatest Thanksgiving of my life this last November. I had driven up to Cook, Minnesota, to visit my dad, Elder Metsa, and share the day with him. The rest of our family had made other holiday plans and had invited us, but due to the weather and Dad's health, we decided to keep it simple between the two of us and 'batch' it. Dad had reserved two meals prepared by the Cook Lions Club (of which he was a proud member and past president). They were serving hundreds of free meals to families in need, hosted at the local Catholic Church.

I entered the church's dining room and saw a full house – families large and small, single men and women, and couples of all ages shoulder to shoulder along the long metal tables, all enjoying turkey, mashed potatoes and gravy, cooked vegetables, buttered rolls, and two choices of pie for dessert. Coordinating and choreographing it all were the loyal and committed members of the Lions Club, resplendent in their yellow vests and gold pins, cooking the dinners, setting up the buffet line, cleaning the tables, and bussing the dishes back to the kitchen to be washed. Nobody went hungry in Cook, or the surrounding area, that day.

I so admired the scene – deeply touched by it, really – and realized why my dad so enjoyed his time in the Lions Club. They were a tight-knit group of friends, many just strangers at first, that shared a common love for the good of the community. It was, and is, as simple and beautiful as that. While I was picking up our two meals to go, I noticed Gary Albertson, publisher of the *Cook News-Herald*, wearing his Green Bay Packers leather jacket. He and my father were good friends – like-minded conservatives, although Elder was really more of an independent who usually voted for character rather than party. He told me he had gotten down on his knees and prayed for 'Our President' the night Obama was elected in 2008. I asked Gary if he would reserve a quarter page in the next week's issue of the newspaper, as I wanted to remind my dad of his wish to write a thank you letter to the people of his adopted town of Cook earlier that spring. Gary asked that I take a picture of Dad to include in the ad. I made our donation, thanked the volunteers, and headed back across the street, through a lovely sprinkling of virgin snowflakes, to Dad's apartment.

Dad had been suffering from emphysema and COPD for the last couple of years (though he had given up smoking at the age of 60). His one room apartment was an octopus maze of oxygen tanks and hoses, which he'd navigate through via his three-wheeled battery-powered scooter. After he wheeled himself across the street to the hospital after an amazingly painful attack of gallstones a few months earlier, instead of calling 911, we from then on referred to it as his 'Finnish ambulance.' My dad was (pardon my French) one tough son of a bitch. Over the years, and especially in his last years, he always summoned and referred to what the Finns call *sisu,* or inner strength, perhaps best defined as determination beyond all reason. He had that in spades, until the very end.

Dad and I set up a card table for our dinner. I helped him clear off the newspapers, bills, letters and cards, and set up a simple dinner setting of two plates, silverware, and 'Finlander blue' coffee cups. We were surrounded by pictures of him and my mother Bess, pictures of him as a kid at Lake Vermilion, pictures of my brother and sisters and all the grandkids and great grandkids, as well as the plaques and gavels he had received as Mayor, City Councilor, and School Board member. Included was my grandfather Emil Metsa's Lion's Club Membership certificate that I had found a few years earlier and had framed. In a way, we were with our family on this holiday. We said a prayer for all of them, and others less fortunate, and enjoyed our dinner, sharing both our apple and blueberry pies for dessert. They had packed us a couple of extra pieces of pie and Dad made sure I brought an extra piece up to our mutual friend David Morton, who lived on the third floor of his apartment building. We spent the rest of the dinner over a cup of coffee and enjoyed small talk man to man, father to son, and best friend to best friend. While truthfully, I don't remember anything we said (small talk, as it is), I will always remember his cadence and pronunciation with that Finnish lilt, the tenor of his voice like the sound of Metsa's ancient rivers over thousands of smooth and polished stones. It was both the sound and spirit of Thanksgiving all that afternoon, and like Bob Marley said, "He who feels it, knows it." Prayer as sound, and sound as prayer.

I told Dad that it was the perfect time to write his thank you letter to the people of Cook. He was excited I had reminded him of that. I told him I needed to get a photograph as well. He asked me to find him his favorite 'Finlander blue' windbreaker. He put in his dentures and spent just the right amount of time combing that glorious head of hair of his, barely streaked with grey. I remembered a Thanksgiving years before at my sister Kathy's house, when we held hands and bowed our heads to pray, and I looked up, noticed his wavy locks, and prayed that when I was his age, my hair would look at least half as good as that. (I hope God heard that.) We wheeled out in front of his apartment door, with the signs above his head that read 'Elder's Place' and 'Another Day in Paradise,' and snapped the shot. He never looked so handsome.

He worked on the letter all evening, and in it thanked all his friends and family; the Cook Lions Club; the hospital; and every employee at every restaurant, bar, local liquor store and bank that he did business with, including the Fortune Bay Casino (we did have to talk him out of willing his scooter to them, and though it would have been a first, told him they could probably afford one on their own). He wished everyone a blessed and happy Christmas, and a healthy and prosperous New Year. He added, of course, "Remember to be kind and make someone happy. And don't forget, God loves you, and so do I!!" (Two exclamation points.) He took extra time writing out his signature six times, in his perfect

Palmer Method-style penmanship, and we picked the best one, had it scanned, and included it at the bottom of the article. I said goodbye to my dad, told him it was the first time that I felt confident I might see him at least one more time, hugged him and kissed him on the cheek, dropped off the letter at the *Cook News-Herald* and made my way back to the Twin Cities. It ran the following week. That Saturday, Dad was rushed to the hospital with a collapsed lung.

My younger brother John (Dad's goalkeeper and guardian angel since he moved to Cook) called me a day into Dad's hospital stay. He told me to come up as soon as I could; things weren't looking good. I headed up that Sunday as soon as I could. I got to the hospital and Dad lay in bed without much movement, with his oxygen tube mustache, surrounded by the pictures of his family, get-well cards, and cookies and candies brought by friends and neighbors for the family and the doctors, nurses and therapists. My nephew Jason and his girlfriend Amanda set up a bed next to him, feeding him soup, wiping his brow, and rubbing his feet and forehead. Nephew John-Paul and his girlfriend flew in from New York. Many of Dad's friends from Cook came to visit in silence, and his neighbors from the Homestead Apartments brought him his mail and their good wishes. My sister Kathy and her husband Al came in from Duluth. Dad was surrounded by love and prayers of healing. I slept next to him one night, and noticed, through dream-inflected eyes, nurses tending to him every couple of hours. I had to get back to work (knowing Dad would have appreciated that) and waited for his Pastor 'PJ' to come. While he was there, the five or six of us there held hands, and I asked PJ to say a prayer. Dad, who was pretty much incommunicado during those last three days, shook his head, indicating "No, I am not ready yet." He wasn't. The next day Jason proposed to his girlfriend Amanda when Dad came to, and that Saturday my girlfriend Amy and I were absolutely delightfully surprised to get a phone call from the 'Thin Finn from Cook, Minn.' Defying all odds, and a doctor's bet, Elder came back to the living.

During that week, his heart had stopped beating. Fortunately, Jason was there holding Elder in his arms. After a minute or two, he came back. I asked him about that during this phone call. He told me, in terms so matter-of-fact I couldn't be surprised, "It was like a dream. All I saw was a white sheet floating in the breeze." That I had never talked to anyone who had visited the Great Beyond (much less that person being my father), I was curious as to what his thoughts were on that. He said, "It taught me something, Paul, and that is, death is not painful." Well, if ever a father's message to his eldest was to be his last, it really could not have been any more profound than this. And in Dad's humble way, simple as well.

A few weeks later, as my girlfriend Amy (whom my dad loved dearly) and her daughter Piper (who had never met Dad but had spoken with him on the phone) made their way to visit Amy's sister in Tofte, Minnesota, through a snowstorm, they went out of their way to visit Dad in the hospital. He was overjoyed. For that I remain forever grateful. For one, that she and Piper would take time to do that, and two, for my dad to meet Amy's lovely daughter. If that is not love, then I do not need to know what love is. For the first time in my life, words – at this moment – fail me.

A month later, Dad had another collapsed lung and was taken by ambulance to the St. Luke's Hospital in Duluth. Coincidentally enough, that is where my mother, Bess Paul, was going to nursing school when she met Elder on a blind date. She later worked at that hospital. I happened to be in Duluth at a meeting the day after he was admitted. I visited him three times during 24 hours. He LOVED the food, and as if the ghost of my mother were visiting, put on almost 10 pounds in five days. The color came back to his eyes, and he had a view of the harbor on Lake Superior. That circle, now in our time, was complete. It was the last time I would see him alive.

My dad's hundred days via Medicare was coming to an end. He had to be transferred to a nursing home. Though my heart ached that there would come a day that he could no longer live independently, he steeled me by telling both me and Amy, "You play the cards you are dealt," and also by saying, in the old-school, last-of-his generation way, "When the band plays a waltz, you don't dance a polka." As a musician, and a son who never doubted his father's words, I accepted that.

My brother John got him a room at the Edgewood Nursing Home in Virginia, his hometown. When I asked my dad how he felt about that, he said sweetly, "It will be like a homecoming." And it was. On March 7 he entered the nursing home. The first person he saw was his ninth grade girlfriend. His Finntown buddy and lifelong friend, Floyd 'Flitch Jaros, was just a few rooms up the hall. His first cousin Irma was there, as were many of his old friends, clients and constituents from the city of Virginia. He received an ovation on his first night at the dinner table. He remarked to my sister Jackie, "What a beautiful place to finish out my life." His room had a view of pine trees and a mine pit. He was eager to see a deer or two on the horizon. Ever the politician, he also told Jackie, "Everyone has their name in big letters on the doors, and if I don't know them, I'll just knock and introduce myself."

He had a great weekend. On Monday morning, March 10, we called him. I was going to be up in Duluth again that Wednesday and was going to drive up to Virginia to see him. I asked him if I could bring him anything. He said, "YES, one of Amy's mother's apple pies!" I told him we'd bring him a fresh one and a frozen one. (Amy's mother, Betty, at 94 years old, can still bake a kick-ass apple pie.) He called my nephew Jordan and asked him to bring him a little brandy. (I apologized ahead of time to the staff of the Edgewood, if this was not allowed.) Jordy guessed correctly on the brand of brandy and brought him a half pint of E & J.

Dad mixed himself a brandy 7, and Jordy played him the new video of my song "Jack Ruby" on his iPad, which Dad had never seen. Breaking a more than 60-year rule of listening to nothing but Jim Reeves, my dad said, "Tell Uncle Paul that is damn good. Damn good!" They visited and Jordy had to leave. Nephew Jason's now fiancée Amanda came up and made him his favorite root beer float. He had Amanda text Allen Cheves, my sister Jackie's oldest son and Elder's first grandson, asking for his address, as Allen's birthday was the following week. Allen texted back the address, and Elder had Amanda put the now-signed birthday card into the envelope, addressed and ready to send. It was 8 p.m. or so. Elder told Amanda he had to get ready for bed and she left. His attendant came in a half hour later to give him his shower. My brother called and said the nursing home had called and said Dad had 'an episode' in the shower. While I was on the phone with him, his other phone rang, to say Dad had passed away. It was just before 9 p.m.

On that Monday night, Jason called. He was in St. Paul serving as the State Representative from District 6B. We drove up together to see Dad for the last time at the funeral home in Cook. We stopped by on Tuesday morning. Elder looked handsome and at peace, not an oxygen tank or tube to be found, hair combed, and in beautiful sleep. Brother John, Jason and I hugged and kissed him, and knelt beside him and said our prayers. We went upstairs to make funeral arrangements. The funeral director, Warren Mlaker, said, "There is not much to take care of. Your dad stopped by on his scooter this summer, on his way back to his apartment from the Montana Café. He saw our door open, swung by, and said, 'I saw you were open and thought I'd make my funeral arrangements.'" All we had to do was figure out the time. We did. And then he said, "Before Elder left, he asked where I went to school. I told him the University of Minnesota. And then Elder asked, "Is there still that Bronze statue of me in front of the women's dormitory?"

Leave it to Dad to not only have the last laugh, but to share it with us. Dad was ready to go, and like he always said, "When I go to sleep at night, I tell God, 'If you are ready, I am ready.'" And he was. He told us, "Grieve a little, but at the funeral, celebrate my life." And so as I grieve and miss our Sunday night phone calls, I sit out on the front porch in the morning with my coffee, petting my dog Blackie, and I remember when we laid our mother down in Greenwood Cemetery in Virginia in '94, and I sang to her. And now I pray to him, as the sun is out and blue sky appearing, "There's a better home awaiting, in the sky, Lord, in the sky."

Hometownfocus.us, April 4, 2014

Paul and (Dad) Elder Metsa
(Photo by Donna Wright)

Thank You

Once again, on this my 84th Thanksgiving Day, I want to thank God for the many blessings I have received. And I also want to sincerely thank so many for being so good and so kind to me. First to my two daughters, Jackie and Kathy and my two sons, Paul and John thank you for loving your Dad and for everything you do for me. And to my nine grandchildren and four great grandchildren thanks for your visits, letters and phone calls.

I also want to convey heartfelt special thanks to the following for you keep me alive with your food, friendship and prayers. Loving hugs to "pj" and friends at St. Paul's Lutheran Church, the Cook Lions Club, the doctors and nurses at the Cook Hospital, employees at American Bank, Zup's, Subway, McDonald's, Franks Pharmacy, Montana Cafe, Crescent Bar & Grill, The Landing, South Switch, Last Chance, Carefree Living, Fortune Bay and the faculty and staff at North Woods School. More hugs to my loving relatives and friends like Don and Shawna, Fred and Bonnie, Roger, Denny, Irm, Carol and Amy, Russ and Linda, Shirley, Becky and Larry, Bud, Bill and Leann, Sue, another Shirley, Mickey and Sharon, Marvin and Sid, Roger and Norene, Ethyl, Judy and Bob, Glady, Gary and Edna, Jennifer, Eileen, Thelma, Lois, Tom, Buddy and Barb, Rocci and Carol, Earl and Irene, Scott and Linda, Carl, Mark and Marg, also Dick Chapman R.I.P. and to those that I forgot!!!

May all of you have a Very Blessed and Merry Christmas and a Happy, Healthy and Prosperous New Year.

Remember to be Kind and make someone Happy. And don't forget, "GOD Loves You and so do I!!"

Elder Metsa

STARS OVER THE PRAIRIE

Back in the days when I was buckshot in short pants
Spinning bottles with Tiger Jack
I remember Grandpa's European prayers
Down in the bunkhouse
To this day I use those prayers to try to bring him back

Hand in hand with my brother and sisters,
Chinese jump rope heart to heart
They ain't hiding,
But they're just out of earshot
Hope to the heavens their worlds don't fall apart

Chorus

(And) I wish I could see stars over the prairie
Stars over the prairie tonight
And I wish I could see
Stars over the prairie
Stars over the prairie tonight

Under the gazebo where I stole my first kisses
In the fallen angel Cadillac with chrome
Where me and my buddies like a good gypsy army
Fighting each other's causes like they were our own

In the greased gravel alleys where I ducked sucker-punches
In the shadow of my old man
Before I blacked out, I wondered how Duke might have done it
Before I found out I took off with the band
Never did go back

Repeat Chorus

There was a Tokyo Rose and a Florida songbird
Loved them both but I could not pick between
They're gone on the downbeat and found true love on
the flipflop
Now all I've got is old love letters and magazines
So, I sit in this city, and I look out my window
Where the neon moons shine when day is done and I see all the
people let it slip through their fingers
You can be with them, but they cannot be with anyone

Repeat Chorus

Words and Music by Paul Metsa
Paul Metsa Music –1984 – BMI ©

AMY

I was just about to write you a poem
that I would read to you
while we sat on your father's broken swing

And when the wind woke
and caused it to sway and swing from side to side
if there were ever sides, as in a perfect world

There aren't
Just birds far above us
that float and glide in all directions

As there are many ways to go
And trust me, nothing but open sky
through windows without curtains
When dusk and dawn, daylight and sundowns
become the perfect moment and most invisible

Out of the closet come all ghosts
that need nothing more than someone braver than them
And then, to become who they are in dance and
silent poetry those songs, those loud guitars
sung in gutters on those nights with one hundred stars

And the rest, in castles, then in clouds some still left to play
And when we find them
I will play both mine, and them for you

DANGEROUS HIGHWAY

Saw a halo of headlights round about midnight
You were broke down on the side of the road
White line before me

Two angels at my side-
One guards my weakness
One tames my pride.

Love is a dangerous highway
Love is a curve that is blind
I should have known you're no roadside attraction
I should have told you this was no regular ride
Stole the ring off my finger when you shook my hand
One angel whispers "love"
"Danger" the next demands

Love is a dangerous highway
Love is a ribbon of sand
I heard the church bells outside of Vegas
I saw the blackbirds from the missions in flight

I drive in silence
and dream of sin
I want to take my baby to where she's never been
Love is a dangerous highway
Love like the road never ends

The neon was fading outside of Reno
She put the ring on my finger, said thanks for the ride
Got a dashboard halo
Flipped a copperhead

Saw three angels
and a sign that read

Love is a dangerous highway
Love like a raincloud ahead
Love is a dangerous highway
that bends like a rainbow she said

By Paul Metsa and Kelly Hotchkiss

BEYOND JERUSALEM

When our lips first touched
And I thought I tasted water
And realized it was wine

From some holy place
Beyond Jerusalem
And closer to home

And a mandolin finally in tune
Played softly, through rain from summer trees
And water was wind, and wind was water

That words were both less and more
And shadows meant nothing
But spoke in ancient words
And the sound of them moved mountains
Slowly like the rhythm of love

Like invisible trains
That all arrive on time

BLACKIE AND PAUL – A DOG AND HIS MAN

I adopted Blackie, a little four-legged, 32-pound Border Collie mix full of goodness, madness, muttness and wonder in the summer of 2003.

A couple months prior to his arrival, my father had fallen down several stairs at his apartment, unknowingly punctured a lung and broken three ribs. He felt pretty weak, and three days later had to be taken by ambulance to St. Mary's Hospital in Duluth, Minnesota, where he ended up in a coma for six weeks. Two or three times a week I'd drive up from Minneapolis to sit by his side, cut his nails, comb his hair, and say prayers to whoever might be listening. "Everything is going to be okay, Dad," I would whisper in his ear. For the most part, he was unresponsive, but there was a fleeting moment when I detected a tear fall from his eye, and I knew that he knew I was there.

This went on for almost eight weeks. In perusing the Duluth News Tribune during my visits, twice a week I'd read ads for the various animal rescue outfits in the Northland. I made a pledge to God and the Universe that if Dad survived this ordeal, I'd adopt a homeless dog to transfer the healing energy.

Miraculously, things began looking up and his oxygen and feeding tubes were removed. Toward the end of August, we were able to get him transferred to a small nursing home facility one hundred miles north in the town of Cook. Though initially he couldn't walk, talk or write his name, thanks to a dedicated team of therapists, nurses and doctors, and a healthy measure of Sisu, Dad made a slow but steady recovery. The day arrived when he was able to move into his own apartment in the three-story complex for seniors across the street. I knew it was time to make good on my pledge.

At that time, my only requirements for a dog were that it be about knee-high and suited to share my home in Northeast Minneapolis. My girlfriend Renea and I made a trip to Contented Critters in Makinen, Minnesota, a predominantly Finnish enclave about 40 miles north of Duluth. Owners Walter and Faye greeted us warmly and gave us a tour of the compound. It was an incredible place, something that could have come out of Dr. Doolittle's fever dream. Among the tenants were a 900-pound hog, a three-legged horse, a blind turtle, feral cats that had the complete run of the place, and perhaps 40 or so dogs, most of them larger hunting dogs, all too big for my house.

We didn't find what we were looking for but wanted to make a donation anyway. As Renea started back to get the checkbook out of my truck, we heard a loud bark from a corner of the property we hadn't checked out. We asked who that was.

"Oh, that's Blackie," Walter replied, "but he has some issues." Well, who doesn't? Curiosity led us across the grounds where we found him in a little kennel. With ears pinned back and brown eyes missing nothing, Blackie was barking as if he knew this might be his chance of redemption. He was right.

Renea asked Walter to open the latch. Watching him step tentatively out from the little wire prison, Renea leaned down and said sweetly, "You don't look so tough." Blackie seemed to sense he was among new friends. He sat on his haunches, stopped barking, and one ear went up, one went down – a configuration which we thereafter referred to as '*The Flying Nun*', after the old Sally Field television series. It was love at first sight.

Walter and Faye filled in the history. Blackie had come into Contented Critters a year before and was immediately adopted by a young farm couple who kept him on a long leash in the yard while they were at work. Two days later, Blackie managed to chew through his leash and took off into the woods where he was on his own through all four seasons of northern Minnesota weather. He quickly became a local legend. There were Blackie sightings at the local dump, in the neighborhood going through garbage cans, and under abandoned vehicles where he sometimes slept. Though many folks tried to catch him, it was a kind lady who kept putting out food and water in her barn who was finally able to capture him. He was then returned to Contented Critters under strict supervision. When we came along, it was like kindred rebel spirits uniting as one.

In mid-October my brother and I were watching the World Series with Dad in his new apartment when Renea called on Wednesday night from Minneapolis with alarming news. She'd been dog-sitting for Blackie when her brother stopped by to visit. As he walked in, Blackie bolted. Out into the dark inner-city night. My heart sunk at the news. I told her I'd leave Cook first thing in the morning.

By the time I got home late Thursday morning, Renea had already put posters up around South Minneapolis. We drove around for several hours to no avail on that afternoon and evening. I was heartbroken. That little guy who'd spent an entire year surviving in the Northwoods was now lost in a tangle of urban strangeness. Sleep came fitfully. I couldn't imagine never seeing him again.

I went home and found two new voicemail messages. The first was from a man who had been out walking his dog when he saw Blackie get hit by a car at a busy intersection in South Minneapolis, about three miles from Renea's house. He stayed with Blackie, saw my phone number on the dog tag, called me, and then called Animal Control. The second message was from Emergency Vet in Golden Valley, where Animal Control had taken Blackie. I called Renea, she came over immediately, and we headed for Emergency Vet.

It was close to 10 p.m. when they brought him out on a blanket. He was pretty beat up – fat lip, very woozy, but alive and breathing. The vet said he'd need to keep Blackie overnight to see if it would be worth saving him, and then asked (and anyone who has ever had a sick pet knows this drill) "Do you have a credit card?" As fate would have it, I had one in my wallet that I'd never activated. With a few clicks, I had $5,000 in credit. But no dog to take home. Entrusting him to the vet for the night, we left feeling hollow but relieved to know he was alive.

Saturday morning we returned to find Blackie sheltered in an oxygen box. Due to a broken pelvis, he couldn't sit up, but still managed to thump his tail in greeting. Then came the Flying Nun thing – one ear up, one down. Message received. I told the doctor to do whatever needed to be done. When I adopted that little guy – a conduit of sorts for my father's healing energy - I wasn't expecting him to reenact the whole damn accident as well, but there was no going back now.

After the team at Golden Valley stabilized him, we drove Blackie to the University of Minnesota Veterinary Hospital for surgery on his broken pelvis and related issues. This required a weeklong stay. We visited daily and kept our fingers crossed for a total recovery.

The long-awaited day finally came when we got the call that Blackie was ready to return home. His little body had been shaved and now revealed a torso of bluish skin, an indication that he had some Australian Blue Healer blood. We wrapped him up comfortably in a warm blanket and took him home.

My bedroom became the convalescence unit. We covered the entire room in plastic and positioned Blackie next to my bed, surrounded by pillows. Every morning, and three times a day, we'd pick him up gently and carry him to the backyard to do his business, then return him to a soft blanket on the porch to enjoy the rays of the sun as the days were getting shorter. In contrast to the loud barking he'd once demonstrated at Contented Critters, he oddly enough never barked the whole time he was in Minneapolis. Our serious bonding had begun. I thought often about my father's long struggle to regain strength at the nursing facility while watching those early times on the porch with Blackie as he tried his best to stand up, but to no avail. My heart broke in little pieces wondering if he would ever walk again.

Then one day, lo and behold, while the sun was out and I was reaching for another sip of coffee, he slowly, though unsteadily, started to stand up. In the warm sunshine of a December morning, with his diaper still secured, he finally succeeded! I was a mess, crying like a new dad who had just seen his baby for the first time. We were now joined at his recovering hips. I guess I should have sensed it, for just days prior to that grand performance, he had barked for the first time out of the blue, a signal that better days were sure to come.

After his recovery, when he was finally able to go for a walk, we were heading down the alley when I slipped on the ice and sprained my ankle. Blackie waited patiently as I struggled to get up. As I limped back home, I realized he was limping, too, mimicking my injury. We were two souls in communion.

This began a 14-year journey of wonder, love, friendship, loyalty, and camaraderie the likes of which I'd never known. Within those four paws of truth and beauty, rescue dogs are the furry embodiment of the second chance. It is nothing less, between dog and man, than truth laid bare. You realize it early on.

Eventually, Renea and I broke up. Ever the faithful companion, the years with Blackie that followed got better, so much better. He knew when I was up and knew when I was down. I'd take him to gigs, put his blanket behind me on the stage, and he'd sleep while I entertained the crowds. Trips to the dog park included counting how many times he'd try and mark his spot. I think the record was 43 times, the last 25 of which he just sprayed air at bystanding trees and bushes. He was never aggressive, nor would he ever back down when approached by a larger or more aggressive dog.

One might say he was fearless, although he did have his quirks. Like the first time my good buddy Cray came to housesit and look after Blackie while I went up North. He came over Saturday afternoon. When I returned on Sunday night, Cray said, "Oh, you must have taken Blackie with you." No. We found him sitting silently behind the recliner in my bedroom, where he'd been the whole time Cray was there, quiet as a mouse. (Roll another one, Cray.)

My father and I had a spring ritual that included grilling streaks on the first visit to our cabin on Lake Vermilion for the opening of fishing season. Dad's go-to was the No Name Steaks – that is, not top of the line, but still tasty. On one such trip, we had three steaks marinating while firing up the grill. It took a while to do that, and by the time we reached around to grab the steaks, they were gone! Blackie had downed two and was working on the third when we discovered the crime.

During our weekly Sunday night calls, Dad would always ask, "How is that steak-eatin' dog of yours?" Though Blackie was a tad skittish towards him in the beginning, it didn't take many visits to the senior apartments before Blackie, off the leash, would lead the way out of the elevator, right to my father's open door in anticipation of treats and pats. Survivors both.

Along with my father, the other love of Blackie's life was Amy. We met in February, 2011, at an outdoor rally I was playing at the Minnesota State Capitol, when she grabbed me by the arm before I did a header into a snowbank after slipping on the ice. I gave her my number, writing it on the back of her protest sign. After searching the internet for my police record, she called me, and we started dating. It began a lovely seven-year relationship and three-way love affair between Amy, Blackie and me.

We spent a lot of time at her place on 35 acres of farmland. Blackie had plenty of room to run and roam, and he adopted her as his mother. He'd be at the door waiting for her to come home from work, greeting her with yelps while jumping up and down. They'd go to visit Amy's mom Betty, who lived six blocks through the woods, and he grew to love her as well. Before his eyesight started to go, he'd often run solo on the path to her front porch and stand by the door until she let him in for treats. Over the years, Blackie and I also played many dog rescue benefits. He was a symbol of hope for dozens of other homeless pups that found their way to other forever homes.

I remember the exact moment I realized Blackie was starting to slow down. We were in Amy's kitchen fixing dinner when I noticed a cloudiness in his eyes. He was developing cataracts. Some say adopting an animal is a 'contract with sorrow.' While my memories of him contradict that, I was reminded of our talks on my back porch when I promised him I would never let him live past his time on this earth, and never ever let him lead a life of pain for my own gratification. We'd still have almost two more years together, but I was reminded to enjoy every day, walk, and laugh with my little hobo dog.

By the spring of 2017, we had to keep an eye on him when we let him outside. His hearing was starting to go, and he was leaving messes in the house. It was so hard to watch this once proud and brilliant dog just simply getting older. It tore at my heart, one string at a time.

Instead of his usual bed of pillows and blankets, we now had to keep him in a small pen by the front door, as it was easier to clean up after him on the linoleum. He still loved to see us in the morning, and those mornings became ever so important.

It was on a Tuesday morning. Amy had already left for work. When I went down to check on Blackie, I could see he was sprawled out on his belly on the floor. I thought perhaps his nails were too long and he had slipped and couldn't get traction to get up. I picked him up gently to place him upright and he fell again. This was not good. I called the vet, Dr. Marie, owner of 3-pound Cat, and told her I had a feeling that it might be time for that house call that no pet owner wants to make. She had treated him a couple of times, once after what might have been a heart attack from which he recovered fully. She suggested I wait 24 hours and see if there was any improvement, calling him "the king of the comeback."

I woke up Wednesday morning hoping for the recovery that never came. Blackie, once again, was lying on his belly on the floor. I took him outside to hold him up while he did his business, exactly like I did 14 years earlier when he was recovering from his accident. Holding him, I felt sand leaving an hourglass, then grabbed my phone and made an appointment with Dr. Marie for Friday at 8 a.m. It was time to see what I was made of, and I wasn't sure if I could handle any of it.

Blackie had been my rock of Gibraltar – when I lost my job, when I found out I was diabetic, through the death of my father. He always knew when I was down or troubled, and had always sidled up next to me, letting me peer deeply into those chocolate brown eyes where it seemed I could look back into the beginning of time and find the psychic secret passageway out of the darkness and madness. He was my crystal ball and good luck charm. He never let me down.

At 4 p.m. Amy came home to take over hospice duties. She, too, was shaken. I packed up my guitar and went to my weekly gig at Shaw's Bar in NE Minneapolis with Wee Willie Walker, my dearest friend and one of the greatest soul singers of our time. Willie loved Blackie, too, and knew what I was going through. That night he sang Bessie Smith's signature song, "Nobody Knows You When You're Down and Out" and dedicated it to "Blackie, the patron saint of all rescue dogs." I played respectfully in time, my head hanging down toward the stage, eyes flooding with tears. It is times like these that music is most important, and my soul was steeled by the support of Willie. By that time, most of the people in the bar knew what I was going through. Bless them all for those silent waves of support. I got several hugs on my way out the door.

I arrived home around 10 p.m. and carried Blackie out to do his business, knowing it might be the last time he'd need to. We were bathed in moonlight and the soft breeze blew the tears off my face, landing on his soft black fur that had slowly turned grey after all those years. I positioned him on a small mattress next to the wall and set up my blankets and pillow next to his. Over the course of the next few hours, he would try to stand up or move, and either caught a paw between the mattress or the wall or ended up in an uncomfortable position. An arm's length away, I'd gently move him to make him as comfortable as possible. Finally, at about 3 a.m., we both fell asleep. I fell into a deep dream that was a technicolor highlight reel of the dozens of times we took walks, enjoying life and each other, with nary a care in the world.

At 6 a.m. I heard Amy coming down the stairs. I felt a warmth next to my side and opened my eyes to find Blackie's snout cradled gently on my shoulder. This guy, who hadn't been able to walk or crawl for two days, had somehow managed to find his way back into my arms. Was it that last rebel burst of energy that had sustained him through that year alone in the woods, or did an angel gently lift him into my arms? I will never know. What it was, was his last and greatest gift to me. Hearts beating side by side, I could feel him signaling me: "Everything is going to be okay, Dad… Even times when my eyes were failing and my hearing going, times when I didn't remember you, you were there for me. Now I am here for you. And in this moment, I want to relieve you of your greatest grief."

We had reached the pinnacle. It was the most beautiful and profound moment of my life. Over the past 14 years, we had developed a telepathy unlike anything I'd ever experienced. Two souls in communion.

Amy and I waited patiently for the vet. We took Blackie out for the last time, and put a small bowl of water next to his snout, from which he took a couple of sips. We held him, rubbed his head, and whispered how much we loved him, never letting him go. Truth be told, he was ready to go, and I think even without the vet's visit, he probably would have flown this earthly coil that day.

The vet arrived promptly at 8 a.m. She kneeled gently and quietly administered the medicine. It took a couple of minutes to take hold as we brushed him – his fur once jet black, now a halo of grey – and held him again, whispering into those Flying Nun ears how much we loved him. He took his last breath knowing we were by his side.

Amy gently washed him and wrapped him up in his favorite ratty purple Mexican blanket and placed him in a wicker basket on the front porch. Out of nowhere, two Sandhill cranes that had a nest across the field came, for the first time, within 20 yards of the house. We watched as they did a slow and ancient mystical dance before disappearing again behind the pine trees. Amy's daughter Piper told us that cranes are considered by Asians and Native Americans in lore as 'echo birds' that help spirits move from one plane to the next. Blackie deserved no less.

It was now time to make good on the rest of that promise I made to him 14 years ago on our back porch, and take him to his resting place under a pine tree and next to the lake.

We said goodbye to Amy and headed north, making our first stop in Hinkley at the Holiday gas station. I pulled up next to a homeless vet who was driving a bicycle, with a small pit bull under a sleeping blanket on the trailer he was pulling, anchored by a small American flag at the back of the trailer. As we were getting coffee together, he told me how he had rescued his dog from a puppy mill. I reached into my wallet, gave him a 20-dollar bill and said, "Keep 10 for yourself, but buy your buddy the largest steak 10 dollars can buy. Tell him it's from Blackie."

As we were driving, I remembered how excited I was going to be to finally have a dog, and envisioned scratching his snout as he sat in the back seat behind me. And here we were, all those years later as he lay behind me, wishing I could scratch that snout just one more time. We finally got to the cabin, and I'd like to think Blackie knew he was home, surrounded by those smells that always transfixed him; those woods where he'd trot merrily on his own, always to return; and a soft mist rising off the lake, welcoming him back.

I found the perfect spot for him, right next to and beneath the branches of a pine tree, and just a whisper distance from the lake with waves, slapping against the rocks, that had put us to sleep dozens of times. I dug a grave through the sand and gravel and opened his blanket for one last hug. I placed inside a handful of my father's ashes, a few good luck charms, guitar picks, and a couple of pictures of him and me. I covered him softly with the sand and gravel and patted down the ground around him. I found the perfect rock to use as his headstone, wrote his name on it with a black marker, and added a small American flag from my mother's jewelry box that still had a lingering scent of her favorite Estée Lauder perfume.

Afterwards I pulled up an old wooden bench – weathered by decades of Vermilion wind, rain and snow – and sat there until the sun went down. The Best of Blackie scenes played over in my head – how two rebel spirits bonded, one with two legs, one with four, sharing a life that you read about in fairy tales. Then I went inside, got under the covers, and cried myself to sleep.

Paul and Blackie
(Photo by Donna Wright)

HAWKEYE

Like all birds that fly above you, I am one of them One
guitar, can it be both wings?
Can I circle the sun, keep both boots in muddy
ground?

And when I sing, can it float off farther into the universe?
to meet only with silence and the beating of wings
of clouds on their way to somewhere else
to hold the first raindrop from a full grey cloud
and say I'm sorry ahead of time
and promise that drop of rain and others land gently on
the ground
to full-throated and running rivers, and a small pond just
to the west
that has only just appeared
with yet a bird around it, but from all, all which will
drink
and fly forward, to where all good birds go
somewhere beyond us, and yet with us in wing and spirit
spotting all below, and teaching wherefore not to land
but to fly above, and let drops of rain and forgiveness
fall freely

When it comes in time, water all that needs to come next in
drops of God's breath, whether you believe or not 'Cause baby
all we need is water, and water matters
most
Let poets and cops figure out the rest

WHAT A DIFFERENCE A DOG MAKES

In the days and weeks after we released Blackie – The Patron Saint of All Rescues – to the Rainbow Bridge, I was adrift and forlorn. He'd been my little buddy for almost 15 years.

When he wasn't at his command post under my desk or in the hall closet, he was literally my shadow. I missed our daily walks, his little dance and yelps when my girlfriend Amy pulled into the driveway after work, and his quiet vigilance as we'd stroll the fields of her farm.

When his hearing and eyesight started to fail, he was content to curl up next to Amy's lovely mom Betty and join us for Sunday night viewings of *Columbo* reruns after dinner. That little 32-pound bundle of joy could light up a room like his canine progenitor Old Hemp and brought smiles wherever he went. The days were empty without him.

Everyone kept telling me to get a new dog. Dog lovers know it's not that easy. I resolved to just let time, space, and silence heal my broken heart. Spring gave way to summer and fall. To the kind friends who urged me to get a new pup, I'd half-heartedly reply," The dog will find me. Like Blackie did."

Fall gave way to winter. Built in 1894, the cracks and crevices in the walls of my old house were havens for small creatures of Nordeast. Every few years, mice would sneak through to escape the snow and cold. Though I sympathize, they are a complete pain in the ass. In late November, a small family of rodents was having its way in my kitchen. I tried mouse traps and pellets of poison, to no avail. It was time to get serious.

I remembered that my friend Cheri Friedman, a tireless advocate on behalf of lost dogs, was hosting an animal adoption the first week of December 2017, at Pet Smart in Maple Grove, an outer ring suburb of Minneapolis. The event was sponsored by Homeward Bound, a rescue operation that Blackie and I had played many a benefit for. What the hell, I figured, might as well peek at the dogs after I perused their website for cats.

I scrolled down, and about the fourth or fifth photo I saw a picture of a little guy named Highway, so named because he was found alongside a highway in Alabama. He had the goofiest smile and seemed to be prancing in place. It was love at first sight. I called Cheri at 11:00 that evening and asked her to put a hold on that guy. I just had that feeling.

I showed up at 10 a.m. on the nose, just as they were opening the doors. There were about 25 dogs in small kennels and cages, all shipped up from Alabama. I walked over and spotted Highway lying in his kennel, having no part of this routine. Although he didn't resist me putting a leash on him, he refused to budge. Pulling gently in hopes that he'd get up, it looked like I was mopping the middle aisle of the store with him. Highway was having no hand, or paws, in the matter.

That was understandable. First, somebody leaves him on the side of a highway; then he gets trucked up to the snowy climes of Minnesota in a large van with 25 other dogs. Add to that the indignity of getting neutered and chipped and sleeping for a month in a strange town, with strange people, and dogs he only knew from the ride.

I finally got him out to the cold grass and petting area in front of the store, sat down, petted him, and introduced myself. Cheri came out to check on us, and I asked her to go back in and see if there was a deal to be had on this canine orphan. In the meantime, I stood up to stretch my legs. A minute later, Highway stood up on his hind legs and gave me my first hug. He found me. Just like Blackie. We were two souls in communion.

There was a guy leaning on the fence surrounding the petting area. I gave him my phone and asked if he'd take our picture together. As fate would have it, I was wearing a Goodwill leather jacket (black, yellow and white) that matched Highway's fur coat perfectly. We could have gone to the prom together dressed like that. As I gave the guy my camera, he asked, "Are you Paul Metsa? I loved your book *Blue Guitar Highway*!"

Words, worlds, and goodwill collide. "Take what you have gathered from coincidence," is my favorite line from Dylan's "It's All Over Now, Baby Blue." Okay, masters of the universe, I get it.

The sun was now out, casting our shadow together. The price tag on this little guy was $400, offsetting the expenses for Homeward Bound folks who had trucked the doggies up from Alabama and housed and fed them for a month. Many dog rescue operations and folks do this as volunteers, paying for expenses out of their own pockets. Trust me, all these folks are angels. But truth be told, I also needed new tires on my truck, another $400 purchase. Cheri came out smiling and said, "Paul, for all the work you and Blackie have done and all the benefits you've played, they'd like to gift the dog to you." I don't know if Highway was crying, but I was.

Cheri loaned me her kennel and I bought a first bag of dog food in months. I loaded the little guy in the back seat and headed home – a new leash on life, you could say, for both of us. He was quiet during the ride and offered no resistance when we arrived. Easing him out, I led him to our back door, opened it, and let him off the leash. Less than a minute later, he'd found his way to my bed, turned over on his back with paws in the air, and let me scratch his belly. Home sweet home. Let the games begin!

I called him Highway for a few days, but it seemed awkward. Laura, wife of my oldest friend, John Pasternacki, suggested I just call him Blue, per our connection. It made perfect sense. On his first visit to the vet, I wrote down his new name: Blue Guitar Highway 61 Metsa, or 'Blue' for short.

These days he can be totally lovable or a handful, sometimes both. Blue has learned to jump a fence, communicate in a series of tonal howls, and keeps me on my toes. He greets visiting friends or neighbors stopping by with equal enthusiasm, his tail wagging like windshield wipers in the pouring rain. He's a hippie; he loves everybody. If dogs could run for office, he could easily be the next

Mayor of Minneapolis; he's that adorable. Due to his newfound ability to sneak out of the back yard, he's even gained a new nickname: Bluedini. Truly, what a difference a dog makes.

One of the joys of my life has been watching my two rescue dogs while they sleep, enjoying the warmth, comfort and safety of their new home. To me, they represent the canine embodiment of Abraham Lincoln's line, offering their owners and others "malice toward none and charity toward all."

The canine formerly known as Highway.
His full name now is Blue Guitar Highway 61 Metsa,
or Blue for short.

BOB DYLAN—HIGHWAY 53 REVISITED

You can walk into an Iron Range bar on the weekend and see any of the five character types imbued in Bob Dylan's persona: the greaser dressed in black leather jacket, white T-shirt with a pack of Lucky Strikes rolled up in his shirtsleeve, dark sunglasses, leather belt buckled on the side, and engineer boots; the hard-working miner fresh off his second shift, enjoying a cold one before going home to the wife and kids; the asshole protesting that his drink is not strong enough and costs too much; the Trickster doing card tricks at the bar and gambling with loaded dice; or perhaps the weirdo in the back booth drinking cheap brandy straight up and reading James Joyce.

Dylan, then Bobby Zimmerman, was an amalgam of these five characters when he moved from Hibbing to Minneapolis. There he hung out with the beatniks who hipped him to Jack Kerouac, Woody Guthrie, Allen Ginsberg, marijuana and more. There he expanded his intellectual curiosity that was first imbued in him by B. J. Rolfzen, his brilliant high school English and Humanities teacher, who impressed on him the power of language. Add the introduction and influence of like-minded folk musicians of his age that were exploring and performing the acoustic folk and blues that became lifelong touchstones. By January of 1961, he was well prepared to hitchhike to New York City with his seeded saddlebag of influences and would soon become Bob Dylan. And who besides an Iron Ranger hitchhikes to NYC in the middle of winter with a guitar?

I was born in the town of Virginia, Minnesota, in 1955, 20 miles east of Hibbing. In my early teens, I'd sometimes hitchhike to Hibbing, stand in front of the door at 2425 7th Avenue, and envision the man that walked out of that door, whose songs influenced American culture and beyond. His shadow influence on me played no small part in my eventually becoming a professional musician.

I've seen Dylan live in concert close to three dozen times. I've enjoyed moments of complete transcendence at many of those shows. There have also been shows when I spent most of my time in the beer garden, wondering if he was singing in German. Even at those less than stellar ramshackle affairs, I was amazed he was getting away with it, and the perversity of them was kind of its own thrill. I've played enough of my own shows over the years to know everybody has an off night or two, and it's always darkest just before the dawn.

As America's greatest living songwriter, with over 600 original songs and thousands of performances behind him, he is both of us and beyond us. I witnessed two Dylan shows at the end of 2019 (Mankato, MN 10/24, Beacon Theater, NYC 12/1). At nearly 80, he was on top of his game and at the peak of his artistic powers, with the ferocity and enthusiasm of a teenager, coupled with the power of a wise old sage. He's an alchemist of the highest order and remains a monumentally creative artist, painting his latest masterpiece in real time.

Drawing on a catalog of songs spanning nearly 60 years, many of which are constantly being rearranged, he plays with those songs like a cat plays with a mouse, teasing them out with a magician's touch. His phrasing rivals Sinatra, and his humor and sense of history hover above them all. He leads America's greatest working rock band like Bob Wills with a velvet bull whip. He plays harmonica like Little Walter with a trunk full of cash in his Cadillac. He could also blow in a soft and sweet staccato that would have seduced Juliet down from the balcony. He played both shows standing at an upright piano, conjuring images of him breaking into the Moose Club on Howard Street in Hibbing to serenade Echo Helstrom, his Girl from the North Country, while the brink of midnight blessed them both by keeping both the cops and moon at bay. The klieg lights of 2019 illuminating the sparkled curtain behind him, silhouetting him in shadow, coupled with various sound effects on his vocals, and his band backing him with impressionistic waves of sound, was pure magic – Laurence Olivier meeting Little Richard on a tightrope, with Billy the Kid holding a net beneath them.

Art in both the smallest and largest of moments, the American Spirit at its core. He is both a man and a concept that has evolved over dozens of reincarnations, withstanding waves of criticism from all corners, and remains unbowed. There is a lesson in that. Steel forged from Iron ore.

At the end of the day – and, in particular, after these shows – it was easy to realize that Dylan and his band could kickstart any VFW or juke joint dance floor anywhere at midnight in America, as he proffers and transmits the ghosts of all that made this country beautiful and, more importantly, mystical, and he is probably fine with that. With his guitar as his lunch pail, off to work he has gone, like any ordinary Joe, for more than 60 years. We are lucky to share this time on earth. And lest we forget, he still has the best hair in the business.

Bob Dylan and band at the Beacon Theatre, New York City, December 1, 2019 (Photo by John Hall)

SLOW JUSTICE

Not all poor men are honest, not all rich men are thieves

But the rich man owns the orchard, and the poor man rakes the leaves

And as the world goes around, all I want to ask is

If the rich man owns the land, why must the poor man pay the taxes?

First Chorus

Why does justice go so slow?

Slow justice slowly goes

Poor means stop, and rich means go

Slow justice slowly goes

They say a woman's work is never done, and do you wonder why?

They get paid half as much for double time on the by and by

I ain't no country doctor, ain't no country doctor's kid

But I'll tell you that my mother never lived in Adam's Rib

Second Chorus

Why does justice go so slow?

Slow Justice slowly goes

Little girl means stop, little boy means go

Slow justice slowly goes

They killed a black minister in Memphis town, a black prince at Audubon Hall

They used different guns in Cape Town, but the same bullet shot them all

South Africa is a ghetto, but it's breaking just like glass

One world with different colors, you know there ain't no second class

Third Chorus

Why does justice go so slow?

Slow justice slowly goes

Any color means stop, only white means go

Slow Justice slowly goes

They will bomb a row of houses, take down the family farm

Shut down all the unions, with the help of the National Guard

Someday those in Congress will have to swallow a bitter pill

They believed Clarence Thomas, but I believed Anita Hill

Repeat First Chorus

Words and Music by Paul Metsa
Paul Metsa Music – 1991 – BMI ©

BLUE

I was left on a highway in Alabama
Just four paws and me
On a highway ridden by those blind
like Helen Keller
And those who wrote like Harper Lee

Those who ran like Jesse Owens
And like Rosa Parks who sat so silently
Like Zelda who married F. Scott Fitzgerald
And Sun Ra louder than cannons on Tripoli

I am both soft and loud like that
Took but one day for you to see
Hearts collide then melt like that
As one, that man dog jubilee

That God he is a funny God
The Universe from A to Z
Who is to ask?
Who really knows?
Matters not to you or me.

Blue's First Christmas
(Photo by Paul)

BLUE GUITAR HIGHWAY

I got my first guitar as an 8-year-old child
She loved me tender, and I held her tight
Days lasted forever, the sky always blue
By my pillow as I slept through the night

I had high flyin' lovers, a ballerina in blue
Moonlight kisses that died on the vine
Some still have their curls, some now lovin' girls
So, I'll sing them this last valentine

Chorus

Blue guitar highway, blue guitar highway
That's where I'm gonna stay
Blue guitar highway, blue guitar highway
That's where I'm gonna stay
On the blue guitar highway

If fame and fortune have been out of reach
I've had enough to carry the day
Friends are my fortune, appeared out of shadows
All along this troubadour's way

Ride along with those campfire cowboys
Beware of bandits in masks and disguise
And if at first you can't kill them with kindness
Then shoot upon the whites of their eyes

Repeat Chorus

Woody Guthrie's the barkeep in Heaven
Gives up the ghost when he closes the bar
So, I'll sing you this tune, 'neath a low hangin' moon
Pennies in fountains goes far

Sundown is coming, dusk turns to a dream
In one hand I hold a picture of mother
and in the other this old true love guitar

Repeat Chorus

Words and Music by Paul Metsa and Kelly Hotchkiss

ABOUT THE AUTHOR

Paul Metsa is a professional musician, guitarist, songwriter, author, radio and television host, social activist, and dog lover. His career includes eight Minnesota Music Awards, over 5,000 professional gigs, forays to Iceland and Siberia (both without international incident) and twelve original recording projects, all of which have gone linoleum. He hosts a weekly radio and television show, both broadcasting out of the Twin Cities. He is also the only musician in America to have played at both the Rock and Roll Hall of Fame in Cleveland (Tribute to Woody Guthrie in 1996) and the United States Hockey Hall of Fame in Eveleth, Minnesota, in 1976. He currently resides in Duluth, Minnesota, with his beloved rescue dog Blue. Paul can be contacted via: https://www.paulmetsa.com

Blue Guitar Highway

Blue Guitar Highway, Paul's autobiography, was published by the University of Minnesota Press in 2011 and is available on Amazon.

New Release

Blood in the Tracks

Paul's next book, *Blood in the Tracks: The Minnesota Musicians behind Bob Dylan's Masterpiece,* co-written with Rick Shefchik, will be published by the University of Minnesota Press in 2023.

Check out Paul's YouTube channel, MetsAmerica, to enjoy his television and radio shows, music videos, and more. Learn more about Paul, purchase his music, and sign up for his newsletter at his website www.paulmetsa.com.

JAN. 1957

"Big Bang." Paul was enchanted the first time he heard his great grandfather Joe Allard playing his wooden flute.

Quick Reference (QR) Code

Here's a QR Code that links you to 14 free songs from the book. If you've not used a QR Code before, it's easy. Use the camera app or other scanner app on your phone to take a snapshot of the code. Follow any instructions that might pop-up on your phone, if necessary, and your phone will open the website browser to the page with the 14 recordings.

These songs are available as a digital download with the purchase of *Alphabet Jazz*. You can also order CDs from https://paulmetsa1.bandcamp.com

1. Paper Tigers
2. Whistling Past the Graveyard* (w/ Paul Mayasich and Sonny Earl)
3. Jack Ruby
4. Walkin' in a Woman's World*
5. Slow Justice
6. Robots on Death Row
7. Automatic Heroes
8. Christmas at Molly's
9. Black Cadillac*
10. Honeymoon in Drag Alley*
11. Ain't Gonna Whistle Dixie Anymore (w/ Willie Walker and Sounds of Blackness)
12. You Can't Be Brave (If You're Not Scared)
13. Blue Guitar Highway
14. Stars Over the Prairie

(*Denotes live tracks)

All Words and Music by Paul Metsa